SPIRITUALIST MANUAL

ISSUED BY THE

NATIONAL SPIRITUALIST ASSOCIATION OF CHURCHES

OF THE

UNITED STATES OF AMERICA
(A RELIGIOUS BODY)

Tel. ADirondack 4-5845
Harlem Botanical Garden
406 LENOX AVENUE Near 130th ST.
NEW YORK 27, NEW YORK

Revision of January, 1955

```
First Edition ..........................Published 1911
Second Revision .......................Published 1921
Third Revision ........................Published 1925
Fourth Revision .......................Published 1928
Fifth Revision ........................Published 1934
Sixth Revision ........................Published 1940
Seventh Revision ......................Published 1944
Eighth Revision .......................Published 1948
Ninth Revision ........................Published 1955
```

Original General Offices of
National Spiritualist Association
Theodore J. Mayer, Late Treasurer of N. S. A.
(Now N.S.A.C.)
Donor of the Building

MORRIS PRATT INSTITUTE
11811 Watertown Plank Road
Milwaukee 13, Wisconsin

Present General Headquarters
National Spiritualist Association of Churches

Harrison D. Barrett, First President of the National Spiritualist Association, elected President at the first Convention, held in Chicago, Ill., September, 1893, and re-elected annually thereafter up to and including the convention of 1906.

Passed on into the Spirit World at Canaan, Maine, January 12, 1911, at the age of 47 years, 10 months and 17 days.

Dr. George B. Warne, Second President of the National Spiritualist Association, elected Vice-President at the 11th Convention in Washington, D. C., and re-elected at each succeeding convention, up to and including the convention of 1906.

Elected President at the 15th convention in Washington, D. C., 1907 and re-elected annually thereafter until 1920, when under the changed constitution he was elected for a term of three years and again re-elected for a term of three years at the Buffalo convention in 1923.

Passed on into the Spirit World in Chicago, Ill., January 22, 1925, in his 74th year.

JOSEPH P. WHITWELL
St. Paul, Minn.

Third President of the N. S. A.: Elected Trustee at the nineteenth annual convention in St. Louis, Mo., in 1911. Was elected Vice-President at the twentieth convention in Dallas, Texas, in 1912 and was re-elected annually thereafter until 1920, when under the changed constitution he was elected for a term of three years. He was again re-elected for a term of three years at the thirty-first annual convention at Buffalo, N. Y., in 1923.

On the transition of the President, Doctor George B. Warne, January 22, 1925, Mr. Whitwell was elected President by the Board. At the 33rd annual convention held in Milwaukee he was elected President for one year to fill out the unexpired term of Dr. George B. Warne.

At the 34th annual convention, held in Toledo, Ohio, 1926 and at each of the following named conventions, Mr. Whitwell was re-elected to office for a term of three years—37th convention in Boston, 1929; 40th in Chicago, 1932; 43rd in Cleveland, 1935; 46th in Indianapolis, 1938; 49th in Los Angeles, 1941. Retired 52nd convention, St. Louis, Mo., 1944 and elected President Emeritus.

CHARLES R. SMITH
Milwaukee, Wis.

Fourth President: Elected Trustee at the 40th annual convention in Chicago, Ill., 1932, for a term of three years. Re-elected as Trustee at the 43rd convention in Cleveland, 1935. On the passing of Vice-President Rev. Thomas Grimshaw, January 1, 1938, was elected by the Board to fill the unexpired term. Was re-elected as Vice-President for a term of three years at each of the following named conventions: 46th convention, Indianapolis, Ind., 1938; 49th convention, Los Angeles, Calif., 1941. Elected President 52nd convention, St. Louis, Mo., 1944; re-elected 55th convention, Detroit, Mich., 1947; re-elected 58th convention Boston, Mass., 1950; re-elected 61st convention Kansas City, Mo., 1953.

This "Manual" is designed to be a Handbook for Ministers, Speakers and Students, but its use is discretionary with them. It is hoped that Spiritualists generally will find it helpful in presenting the teachings of Spiritualism; and that in sections of our country where there are few spiritualists, and no Mediums or Speakers, it will be an aid to willing workers in holding regular meetings and other services, exclusive of marriage.

NATIONAL SPIRITUALIST ASSOCIATION
OF CHURCHES
of the
UNITED STATES OF AMERICA

Constitutional Convention
National Spiritualist Association

The National Spiritualist Association of the U. S. A. was organized in Chicago, Ill., in 1893. The first convention of the Association was held at No. 77 Thirty-first Street, Chicago, on Sept. 27th, 28th, 29th of that year.

The convention was called to order by Milan C. Edson of Washington, D. C., at 12:40 P.M., Sept. 27th. After the reading of the call for the convention, Milan C. Edson, who was chairman of the calling committee and Robert A. Dimmick, secretary, were elected temporary chairman and secretary of the convention.

Pursuant to the recommendation of the committee on nominations, the following were elected permanent officers of the convention: Harrison D. Barrett, of Lily Dale, N. Y., chairman; Hon. L. V. Moulton, of Grand Rapids, Mich., Vice-President; W. H. Bach, of St. Paul, Minn., Secretary.

When the time arrived for the election of officers, Harrison D. Barrett was elected President by acclamation. Mrs. Cora L. V. Richmond, of Chicago, was elected Vice-President, by the unanimous ballot of the convention.

Two names having been placed in nomination for Secretary, namely, Robert A. Dimmick and E. B. Fairchild, ballots were prepared and the number of votes cast by the delegates was 162. Of those Robert A. Dimmick received 91 votes and E. B. Fairchild 71 votes. R. A. Dimmick was declared elected.

The unanimous ballot of the convention was then cast by the Secretary for Theodore J. Mayer for the office of Treasurer.

Milan C. Edson was then elected by acclamation as First Trustee.

James B. Townsend was unanimously elected Second Trustee.

Mrs. I. N. Sloper of California, upon ballot being taken, was declared elected Third Trustee, the vote afterwards being made unanimous.

Mrs. Marion H. Skidmore of Lily Dale, N. Y., was elected by acclamation as Fourth Trustee.

Geo. P. Colby of Lake Helen, Fla., was unanimously elected Fifth Trustee.

Conventions of
National Spiritualist Association of Churches
Where Held
And Officers Elected

President	Secretary	Treasurer
	1—Chicago, 1893	
Harrison D. Barrett	Robert A. Dimmick	Theodore J. Mayer
	2—Washington, 1894	
Harrison D. Barrett	Francis B. Woodbury	Theodore J. Mayer
	3—Washington, 1895	
Harrison D. Barrett	Francis B. Woodbury	Theodore J. Mayer
	4—Washington, 1896	
Harrison D. Barrett	Francis B. Woodbury	George S. Clendaniel
	5—Washington, 1897	
Harrison D. Barrett	Francis B. Woodbury	George S. Clendaniel
	6—Washington, 1898	
Harrison D. Barrett	Mary T. Longley	Theodore J. Mayer
	7—Chicago, 1899	
Harrison D. Barrett	Mary T. Longley	Theodore J. Mayer
	8—Cleveland, 1900	
Harrison D. Barrett	Mary T. Longley	Theodore J. Mayer
	9—Washington, 1901	
Harrison D. Barrett	Mary T. Longley	Theodore J. Mayer
	10—Boston, 1902	
Harrison D. Barrett	Mary T. Longley	Theodore J. Mayer
	11—Washington, 1903	
Harrison D. Barrett	Mary T. Longley	Theodore J. Mayer
	12—St. Louis, 1904	
Harrison D. Barrett	Mary T. Longley	Theodore J. Mayer
	13—Minneapolis, 1905	
Harrison D. Barrett	Mary T. Longley	Theodore J. Mayer
	14—Chicago, 1906	
Harrison D. Barrett	Mary T. Longley	Theodore J. Mayer
		Cassius L. Stevens

CONVENTIONS 17

President	Secretary	Treasurer
	15—Washington, 1907	
Dr. George B. Warne	George W. Kates	Cassius L. Stevens
	16—Indianapolis, 1908	
Dr. George B. Warne	George W. Kates	Cassius L. Stevens
	17—Rochester, 1909	
Dr. George B. Warne	George W. Kates	Cassius L. Stevens
	18—San Francisco, 1910	
Dr. George B. Warne	George W. Kates	Cassius L. Stevens
	19—St. Louis, 1911	
Dr. George B. Warne	George W. Kates	Cassius L. Stevens
	20—Dallas, 1912	
Dr. George B. Warne	George W. Kates	Cassius L. Stevens
	21—Chicago, 1913	
Dr. George B. Warne	George W. Kates	Cassius L. Stevens
	22—Boston, 1914	
Dr. George B. Warne	George W. Kates	Cassius L. Stevens
	23—Rochester, 1915	
Dr. George B. Warne	George W. Kates	Cassius L. Stevens
	24—St. Paul, 1916	
Dr. George B. Warne	George W. Kates	Cassius L. Stevens
	25—New York, 1917	
Dr. George B. Warne	George W. Kates	Cassius L. Stevens
	26—St. Louis, 1918 No Convention held.	
Dr. George B. Warne	George W. Kates	Cassius L. Stevens
	27—Pittsburgh, 1919	
Dr. George B. Warne	George W. Kates	Cassius L. Stevens
	28—Columbus, 1920	
Dr. George B. Warne	George W. Kates	Cassius L. Stevens
	29—Detroit, 1921	
Dr. George B. Warne	George W. Kates	Cassius L. Stevens
	30—Chicago, 1922	
Dr. George B. Warne	Harry P. Strack	Cassius L. Stevens

CONVENTIONS

President	Secretary	Treasurer
	31—Buffalo, 1923	
Dr. George B. Warne	Harry P. Strack	Cassius L. Stevens
	32—Los Angeles, 1924	
Dr. George B. Warne	Harry P. Strack	Cassius L. Stevens
	33—Milwaukee, 1925	
Joseph P. Whitwell	Harry P. Strack	F. W. Constantine
	34—Toledo, 1926	
Joseph P. Whitwell	Harry P. Strack	F. W. Constantine
	35—San Antonio, 1927	
Joseph P. Whitwell	Harry P. Strack	F. W. Constantine
	36—Indianapolis, 1928	
Joseph P. Whitwell	Harry P. Strack	F. W. Constantine
	37—Boston, 1929	
Joseph P. Whitwell	Harry P. Strack	Frank Joseph
	38—Detroit, 1930	
Joseph P. Whitwell	Harry P. Strack	Frank Joseph
	39—Kansas City, 1931	
Joseph P. Whitwell	Harry P. Strack	Frank Joseph
	40—Chicago, 1932	
Joseph P. Whitwell	Harry P. Strack	Frank Joseph
	41—Pittsburgh, 1933	
Joseph P. Whitwell	Harry P. Strack	Frank Joseph
	42—Syracuse, 1934	
Joseph P. Whitwell	Harry P. Strack	Frank Joseph
	43—Cleveland, 1935	
Joseph P. Whitwell	Harry P. Strack	Frank Joseph
	44—Milwaukee, 1936	
Joseph P. Whitwell	Harry P. Strack	Frank Joseph
	45—Fort Worth, 1937	
Joseph P. Whitwell	Harry P. Strack	Frank Joseph
	46—Indianapolis, 1938	
Joseph P. Whitwell	Harry P. Strack	Frank Joseph

CONVENTIONS

President	Secretary	Treasurer
	47—Detroit, 1939	
Joseph P. Whitwell	Harry P. Strack	Frank Joseph
	48—Chicago, 1940	
Joseph P. Whitwell	Harry P. Strack	Frank Joseph
	49—Los Angeles, 1941	
Joseph P. Whitwell	Harry P. Strack	Frank Joseph
	50—Rochester, 1942	
Joseph P. Whitwell	Harry P. Strack	Emil C. Reichel
	51—Chicago, 1943	
Joseph P. Whitwell	Harry P. Strack	Emil C. Reichel
	52—St. Louis, 1944	
Charles R. Smith	Harry P. Strack	Emil C. Reichel
	53—Columbus, 1945	
Charles R. Smith	Harry P. Strack	Emil C. Reichel
	54—Seattle, 1946	
Charles R. Smith	Emil C. Reichel	Harold P. Courtney
	55—Detroit, 1947	
Charles R. Smith	Emil C. Reichel	Harold P. Courtney
	56—Milwaukee, 1948	
Charles R. Smith	Emil C. Reichel	Clyde A. Dibble
	57—San Antonio, 1949	
Charles R. Smith	Emil C. Reichel	Clyde A. Dibble
	58—Boston, 1950	
Charles R. Smith	Emil C. Reichel	Clyde A. Dibble
	59—Indianapolis, 1951	
Charles R. Smith	Emil C. Reichel	Clyde A. Dibble
	60—Tulsa, 1952	
Charles R. Smith	Emil C. Reichel	Clyde A. Dibble
	61—Kansas City, 1953	
Charles R. Smith	Emil C. Reichel	Clyde A. Dibble
	62—Buffalo, 1954	
Charles R. Smith	Emil C. Reichel	Clyde A. Dibble

Officers Who Have Been Elected or Appointed and Who Have Served as Trustees of the

National Spiritualist Association of Churches

HARRISON D. BARRETT

First President of the N. S. A.: Elected President at the first convention, held in Chicago, Ill., in 1893. Re-elected each succeeding year up to and including the year 1906.

Passed into the higher life at Canaan, Maine, Jan. 12, 1911, at the age of 47 years.

DR. GEORGE B. WARNE
Chicago, Ill.

Second President of the N. S. A.: Elected Vice-President at the 11th annual convention, held in Washington, D. C., 1903. Re-elected Vice-President at each succeeding convention up to and including the year 1906.

Elected President at the 15th annual convention, held in Washington, D. C., 1907, and annually thereafter until 1920, when under the changed constitution he was elected for a term of three years at the 28th convention, Columbus, Ohio, 1920 and re-elected for a term of three years at the 31st convention, Buffalo, N. Y., 1923.

Passed to the higher life during his last term of office January 22, 1925.

JOSEPH P. WHITWELL
St. Paul, Minn.

Third President of the N. S. A.: Elected Trustee at the nineteenth annual convention in St. Louis, Mo., in 1911. Was elected Vice-President at the twentieth convention in Dallas, Texas, in 1912, and was re-elected annually thereafter until 1920, when under the changed constitution he was elected for a term of three years. He was again re-elected for a term of three years at the thirty-first annual convention at Buffalo, N. Y., in 1923.

On the transition of the President, Doctor George B. Warne, January 22, 1925, Mr. Whitwell was elected President by the Board. At the 33rd annual convention held in Milwaukee he was elected President for one year to fill out the unexpired term of Dr. George B. Warne.

At the 34th annual convention, held in Toledo, Ohio, 1926 and at each of the following conventions, Mr. Whitwell was re-elected to office for a term of three years—37th convention in Boston, 1929, 40th in Chicago, 1932. 43rd in Cleveland, 1935; 46th in Indianapolis, 1938; 49th in Los Angeles, 1941. Retired 52nd convention St. Louis, 1944 and elected President Emeritus.

CHARLES R. SMITH
Milwaukee, Wis.

Fourth President N. S. A. C.: Elected Trustee at the 40th annual convention in Chicago, Ill., 1932, for a term of three years. Re-elected as Trustee at the 43rd convention in Cleveland, 1935. On the passing of Vice-President Rev. Thomas Grimshaw, January 1, 1938, was elected by the Board to fill the unexpired term. Was re-elected as Vice-President for a term of three years at each of the following named conventions: 46th convention, Indianapolis, Ind., 1938; 49th convention, Los Angeles, Calif., 1941.

Elected President 52nd convention St. Louis, Mo., 1944; re-elected 55th convention Detroit, Mich., 1947; re-elected 58th convention Boston, Mass., 1950; re-elected 61st convention Kansas City, Mo., 1953.

CORA L. V. RICHMOND

Vice-President: Elected at the first convention in Chicago, Ill., 1893. Served as Vice-President for five years, being re-elected 1894, 1895, 1896, 1899.

HON. A. H. DAILY
Brooklyn, N. Y.

Vice-President: Elected at the sixth convention in Washington, D. C., 1898. Served in that office for one term.

H. W. RICHARDSON
East Aurora, N. Y.

Vice-President: Elected at the seventh convention in Chicago, Ill., 1899. Served in that office for one year.

HON. THOS. M. LOCKE
Philadelphia, Pa.

Vice-President: Elected at the eighth convention in Cleveland, Ohio, 1900. Served three terms, being re-elected 1901, 1902.

OFFICERS

HON. CHAS. R. SCHIRM
Baltimore, Md.

Vice-President: Elected at the fifteenth convention in Washington, D. C., 1907. Served for five years, being re-elected each succeeding year up to and including the convention of 1911.

REV. THOMAS GRIMSHAW
St. Louis, Mo.

Vice-President: Elected Trustee at the eleventh convention Washington, D. C., 1903, was re-elected in 1904, 1905, 1906. He was again elected as Trustee in 1908 and at each succeeding convention up to and including 1916. Was again elected in 1920 for a term of one year. At the twenty-ninth convention in Detroit, 1921, he was elected for a term of three years and was re-elected at the thirty-second convention in Los Angeles, 1924, for a term of three years.

On the passing of President Doctor George B. Warne, January 22, 1925, Rev. Thomas Grimshaw was elected Vice-President by the Board. At the thirty-third annual convention held in Milwaukee, Wis., 1925, he was elected Vice-President, for one year, to fill out the unexpired term of Joseph P. Whitwell.

At the 34th annual convention, held in Toledo, Ohio, 1926 and at each of the following named conventions, Mr. Grimshaw was re-elected to office for a term of three years:—37th convention in Boston, 1929; 40th convention in Chicago, 1932; 43rd convention in Cleveland, 1935.

Mr. Grimshaw passed into the higher life during his last term of office on January 1, 1938, at the age of seventy-one years.

REV. ROBERT J. MACDONALD
Rochester, N. Y.

Vice-President: Appointed by the National Board on the passing of Rev. A. Cervin, November 7, 1940. Elected for one year to fill out unexpired term of Rev. A. Cervin, at forty-ninth convention, Los Angeles, Calif., 1941, re-elected for a term of three years at fiftieth convention, Rochester, N. Y., 1942. Resigned as trustee at the 52nd convention, St. Louis, Mo., 1944, and elected Vice-President for a term of three years; re-elected 55th convention, Detroit, Mich., 1947; re-elected 58th convention, Boston, Mass., 1950; re-elected 61st convention, Kansas City, 1953.

ROBERT A. DIMMICK
Washington, D. C.
Secretary: Elected at the first convention in Chicago, Ill., 1893, and served for one year.

FRANCIS B. WOODBURY
Roxbury, Mass.
Secretary: Elected at second convention in Washington, D. C., 1894 and served four terms, being re-elected in 1895, 1896, 1897.

MARY T. LONGLEY
Los Angeles, Calif.
Secretary: Elected at the sixth convention in Washington, D. C., 1898. She served for nine years, being re-elected at each succeeding convention up to and including the fourteenth convention in Chicago, Ill., in 1906. The following year she was elected Trustee at the fifteenth convention in Washington, D. C., serving as Trustee for one year.

GEORGE W. KATES
Rochester, N. Y.
Secretary: Elected Trustee at the ninth convention in Washington, D. C., 1901, was re-elected at Boston in 1902.

Secretary: Elected at the fifteenth convention in Washington, D. C., 1907 and annually thereafter until 1920, when, under the changed constitution, he was elected for a term of two years, but passed to the higher life on September 5, 1922.

I. C. I. Evans was appointed Acting Secretary for the unexpired term.

HARRY P. STRACK
Sandusky, Ohio
Secretary: Elected at the thirtieth annual convention in Chicago, 1922. He was re-elected to office for a term of three years at each of the following named conventions: 33rd convention in Milwaukee, Wis., 1925; 36th convention in Indianapolis, Ind., 1928; 39th convention in Kansas City, Mo., 1931; 42nd convention in Syracuse, 1934; 45th convention in Fort Worth, Texas, 1937; 48th convention in Chicago, Ill., 1940; 51st convention in Chicago, Ill., 1943.

EMIL C. REICHEL
Milwaukee, Wis.

Secretary: Elected Treasurer for a term of three years at the fiftieth annual convention, Rochester, N. Y., 1942. Re-elected 53rd convention, Columbus, Ohio, 1945. Resigned at 54th convention, Seattle, Washington, 1946 and elected Secretary for a term of three years. Re-elected 57th convention San Antonio, Texas, 1949; re-elected 60th convention Tulsa, Okla., 1952.

THEODORE J. MAYER
Washington, D. C.

Treasurer: Elected at the first convention in Chicago, Ill., 1893, was re-elected at the conventions of 1894 and 1895.

Later he was again elected Treasurer at the sixth convention in Washington, D. C., 1898 and was re-elected at each succeeding convention up to and including the convention of 1906.

Mr. Mayer passed into the higher life on March 12, 1907. Mr. Cassius L. Stevens was appointed by the Board to fill the unexpired term of office.

GEORGE S. CLENDANIEL
Washington, D. C.

Treasurer: Elected at the fourth convention, in Washington, D. C., 1896 and was re-elected in 1897.

CASSIUS L. STEVENS
Pittsburgh, Pa.

Treasurer: Elected Trustee at the eighth convention in Cleveland, Ohio, in 1900; was re-elected at each succeeding convention up to and including 1906. In March, 1907, he was appointed by the Board to fill out the unexpired term of Theodore J. Mayer, Treasurer, who passed into the higher life March 12, 1907.

Elected Treasurer at the fifteenth convention, in Washington, D. C., in 1907 and annually thereafter until 1921, when under the changed constitution he was elected for a term of three years, being again re-elected for a term of three years at the thirty-second convention in Los Angeles, Cal., in 1924, but passed into the higher life April 30, 1925.

FREDERICK W. CONSTANTINE
Buffalo, N. Y.

Treasurer: Elected Trustee at the thirty-second convention in Los Angeles, Cal., 1924, for a term of three years.

On the passing of Treasurer Stevens April 30, 1925, he was appointed Treasurer by the Board.

He was elected Treasurer at the Milwaukee convention in 1925 for a term of two years, and re-elected at the San Antonio convention in 1927 for a term of three years, but resigned from office at the time of the thirty-seventh convention, Boston, 1929.

REV. FRANK JOSEPH
Chicago, Ill.

Treasurer: Elected for one year at the thirty-seventh annual convention, Boston, Mass., 1929, to fill out the unexpired term of Fred W. Constantine (resigned) and was re-elected for a term of three years at each of the following named conventions: thirty-eighth convention, Detroit, Mich., 1930; forty-first convention, Pittsburgh, Pa., 1933; forty-fourth convention, Milwaukee, Wis., 1936; forty-seventh convention, Detroit, Mich., 1939.

HAROLD P. COURTNEY
Los Angeles, Cal.

Treasurer: Elected Trustee at thirty-third annual convention, Milwaukee, Wis., 1925, for a term of three years and re-elected at each of the following named conventions: thirty-sixth convention, Indianapolis, Ind., 1928; thirty-ninth convention, Kansas City, Mo., 1931; forty-second convention, Syracuse, N. Y., 1934; forty-fifth convention, Fort Worth, Texas, 1937; forty-eighth convention, Chicago, 1940; fifty-first convention, Chicago, 1943. Elected Treasurer 54th convention, Seattle, Washington, 1946, for term of three years.

CLYDE A. DIBBLE
Burlingame, Cal.

Treasurer: Elected at the 56th annual convention, Milwaukee, Wis., for a term of three years; re-elected at the 59th convention, Indianapolis, Ind.; re-elected at the 62nd convention, Buffalo, N. Y., 1954.

MILAN C. EDSON
Washington, D. C.

Trustee: Elected at the first convention, Chicago, Ill., 1893. He served for three years, being re-elected, 1894 and 1895.

JAMES B. TOWNSEND
Lima, Ohio

Trustee: Elected at the first convention, Chicago, Ill., in 1893; he served for two terms, being re-elected in 1894.

ELIZABETH SLOPER
San Francisco, Cal.

Trustee: Elected at the first convention, Chicago, Ill., 1893, but in April, 1894, resigned. Olive A. Blodgett of Davenport, Iowa, was appointed to fill the vacancy.

MARION H. SKIDMORE
Lily Dale, N. Y.

Trustee: Elected at the first convention, Chicago, Ill., 1893, and served for one term.

GEORGE P. COLBY
Lake Helen, Fla.

Trustee: Elected at the first convention, Chicago, Ill., 1893, but on December 21, 1893, resigned from office. B. B. Hill of Philadelphia was appointed by the Board to fill the vacancy.

B. B. HILL
Philadelphia, Pa.

Trustee: Appointed by the Board as Trustee to fill out term of George P. Colby, who had resigned; was elected Trustee at the second convention in Washington, D. C., 1894 and was re-elected in 1895.

HON. L. V. MOULTON
Grand Rapids, Mich.

Trustee: Elected at the second convention, Washington, D. C., 1894; he served four terms, being re-elected in 1895. 1896, 1897.

OLIVE A. BLODGETT
Davenport, Iowa

Trustee: Elected at the second convention in Washington, D. C., 1894. Shortly after being elected Mrs. Blodgett passed into the higher life.

Mrs. F. C. Stinehart, Dubuque, Iowa, was appointed by the Board April, 1895, to fill the vacancy.

GEORGE A. FULLER
Worcester, Mass.

Trustee: Elected at the third convention in Washington, D. C., 1895, he served for three terms, being re-elected in 1896, 1897.

ABBY L. PETTENGILL
Cleveland, Ohio

Trustee: Elected at the third convention in Washington, D. C., 1895, was re-elected in 1896.

FREDERICK FICKEY, JR.
Baltimore, Md.

Trustee: Elected at the fourth convention, Washington, D. C., in 1896.

HENRY STEINBERG
Washington, D. C.

Trustee: Elected at the fourth convention, Washington, D. C., 1896.

ALLEN FRANKLIN BROWN
San Antonio, Texas

Trustee: Elected at the fifth convention, Washington, D. C., 1897, served two terms, being re-elected in 1898.

H. W. RICHARDSON
East Aurora, N. Y.

Trustee: Elected at the fifth convention in Washington, D. C., 1897.

COL. C. N. STOCKWELL
Nashville, Tenn.

Trustee: Elected at the fifth convention, Washington, D. C., 1897.

OFFICERS

D. P. DEWEY
Grand Blanc, Mich.

Trustee: Elected at the sixth convention, Washington, D. C., 1898; he served for three terms, being re-elected in 1899, 1900.

C. D. PRUDEN
Minneapolis, Minn.

Trustee: Elected at the sixth convention, Washington, D. C., 1898, served five terms, being re-elected in 1899, 1900, 1901, 1902.

MILTON C. BARNARD
Washington, D. C.

Trustee: Elected at the sixth convention, Washington, D. C., 1898, but declined to serve.

I. C. I. Evans of Washington, D. C., was appointed by the Board to fill vacancy.

ERVIN A. RICE
Chicago, Ill.

Trustee: Elected at the sixth convention, Washington, D C., 1898. Later he resigned and Mrs. Emma Nickerson Warne was appointed by the Board to fill the vacancy.

I. C. I. EVANS
Washington, D. C.

Trustee: Appointed by the Board in 1898 to fill the term of Milton C. Barnard, who declined to serve; he was elected Trustee at the seventh convention, Chicago, Ill., 1899 and annually thereafter until 1921, when under the changed constitution he was elected at the twenty-ninth convention, Detroit, Mich., 1921, for a term of three years.

ALONZO M. THOMPSON
Fullerton, Neb.

Trustee: Elected at the seventh convention, Chicago, Ill., 1899, served five successive terms, being re-elected 1900, 1901, 1902, 1903.

F. W. BOND
Willoughby, Ohio

Trustee: Elected at the seventh convention, Chicago, Ill., 1899, served as trustee for one year.

OFFICERS

CARRIE E. S. TWING
Westfield, N. Y.

Trustee: Elected at the eleventh convention, Washington, D. C., served four terms, being re-elected 1904, 1905, 1906.

STEPHEN D. DYE
Los Angeles, Cal.

Trustee: Elected at the twelfth convention, St. Louis, Mo., 1904; he was re-elected in 1905, but passed into the higher life during his second term of office. Arthur S. Howe was appointed to fill the vacancy.

ARTHUR S. HOWE
Los Angeles, Cal.

Trustee: After filling out the unexpired term of Stephen D. Dye, deceased, was elected Trustee at the fourth convention, Chicago, Ill., 1906.

JOHN S. MAXWELL
Minneapolis, Minn.

Trustee: Elected at fifteenth convention, Washington, D. C., 1907, served four terms, being re-elected 1908, 1909, 1910 and was again re-elected by the San Antonio convention 1927 for a term of three years. (Passed to the higher life August 11, 1929.)

ELIZABETH HARLOW GOETZ
Haydenville, Mass.

Trustee: Elected as Elizabeth Harlow at the fifteenth convention in Washington, D. C., 1907, was re-elected in 1908, 1909.

As Mrs. Elizabeth Harlow Goetz, she was again elected Trustee at the eighteenth convention in San Francisco, Cal., 1910 and was re-elected at each succeeding convention up to and including twenty-seventh convention, Pittsburgh, 1919.

On the passing of Treasurer Stevens, April 30, 1925, Mrs. E. H. Goetz was again appointed Trustee by the Board and was re-elected at the Milwaukee convention, 1925, for two years.

On the passing of Rev. Elizabeth Schauss on June 13, 1937, she was appointed Trustee by the Board and was unanimously elected at the forty-fifth annual convention, Fort Worth, 1937 to fill the unexpired term of two years of Rev. Schauss and was re-elected at the forty-seventh convention, Detroit, 1939, for a term of three years.

ALFONSO W. BELDEN
San Diego, Cal.

Trustee: Elected at the fifteenth convention, Washington, D. C., 1907; he served for four terms, being re-elected in 1908, 1909, 1910.

He was again elected in 1911, but resigned at the close of the convention. Josephine A. Bruer, Sterling, Kansas, was appointed to fill the vacancy.

ALONZO M. GRIFFIN
Chicago, Ill.

Trustee: Elected at the twentieh convention, Dallas, Texas, 1912 and annually thereafter until 1920, when under the changed constitution he was elected for a term of three years and was again re-elected for a term of three years at the thirty-first convention Buffalo, N. Y., in 1923. Passed away on the floor of the thirty-fifth annual convention, San Antonio, Texas, October 12, 1927.

DR. OTTO VIERLING
St. Louis, Mo.

Trustee: Elected at twentieth convention, Dallas, Texas, 1912, served three terms, being re-elected 1913, 1914. Passed away St. Louis, Mo., October 1, 1943.

DELVON A. HERRICK
Rochester, N. Y.

Trustee: Elected at the twenty-third convention, Rochester, N. Y., 1915 and annually thereafter until 1920, when under the changed constitution he was elected for a term of two years and again re-elected at the thirtieth convention, Chicago, Ill., 1922, for a term of three years. Passed away, Los Angeles, Cal., January 14, 1938.

HON. MARK A. BARWISE
Bangor, Maine

Trustee: Elected at the twenty-fifth convention, New York City, 1917 and annually thereafter until 1920, when under the changed constitution he was elected for a term of two years and was re-elected at each of the following conventions for a term of three years, thirtieth, Chicago, 1922, thirty-third, Milwaukee, 1925, thirty-sixth, Indianapolis, 1928. Passed away June 3, 1937, Bangor, Maine.

ELIZABETH SCHAUSS
Toledo, Ohio

Trustee: Appointed by the Board to fill vacancy occasioned by the passing of Dr. George B. Warne, President, January 22, 1925. Elected by the Milwaukee convention, 1925 for a term of two years and re-elected for a term of three years at each of the following conventions, thirty-fifth, San Antonio, 1927; thirty-eighth, Detroit, 1930; forty-first, Pittsburgh, 1933; forty-fourth, Milwaukee, 1936. Passed away during her last term of office, June 13, 1937, Toledo, Ohio.

FRED E. STIVERS
Los Angeles, Cal.

Trustee: Elected at thirty-fourth annual convention, Toledo, Ohio, 1926, for a term of three years and re-elected at the thirty-seventh convention Boston, 1929, for a term of three years. Passed away, Los Angeles, December 7, 1937.

REV. A. CERVIN
Taylor, Texas

Trustee: Elected at the thirty-eighth annual convention, Detroit, 1930, for a term of three years and re-elected for a term of three years at each of the following conventions, forty-first, Pittsburgh, Pa., 1933; forty-fourth, Milwaukee, 1936; forty-seventh, Detroit, 1939. Passed away during his term of office, November 7, 1940.

JOHN R. NORGRAVE
Roxbury, Mass.

Trustee: Elected at thirty-seventh annual convention, Boston, Mass., 1929, for one year to fill out unexpired term of John S. Maxwell, who passed away August 11, 1929.

OFFICERS

DR. B. F. CLARK
Indianapolis, Ind.

Trustee: Elected at thirty-ninth annual convention, Kansas City, Mo., 1931, for a term of three years and re-elected for a term of three years at each of the following named conventions: forty-second, Syracuse, N. Y., 1934; forty-fifth, Fort Worth, Texas, 1937; forty-eighth, Chicago, Ill., 1940; fifty-first, Chicago, Ill. Elected for a term of three years at the 58th, Boston, Mass., 1950. Re-elected at the 61st, Kansas City, Mo., 1953.

J. C. BUCHHOLZ
Columbus, Ohio

Trustee: Elected by the National Board on the passing of Rev. Thomas Grimshaw, January 1, 1938 and re-elected for a term of three years at each of the following named conventions: forty-sixth, Indianapolis, Ind., 1938; forty-ninth, Los Angeles, Calif., 1941. (Resigned to serve in the Armed Forces October, 1943.)

RUSSEL S. WALDORF
Springfield, Ohio

Trustee: Elected for a term of one year to fill out the unexpired term of J. C. Buchholz (resigned), at fifty-first convention, Chicago, Ill., 1943. Re-elected at fifty-second convention, St. Louis, Mo., 1944 and at fifty-fifth, Detroit, Mich., 1947, for a term of three years.

REV. VICTORIA BARNES, M.D.
Chicago, Ill.

Trustee: Elected for a term of three years at the 50th annual convention, Rochester, N. Y., 1942. Re-elected at the 53rd, Columbus, Ohio, 1945. Re-elected at the 56th, Milwaukee, Wis., 1948. Re-elected at the 59th, Indianapolis, Ind., 1951. Re-elected at the 62nd, Buffalo, N. Y., 1954.

REV. HUGH GORDON BURROUGHS
Washington, D. C.

Trustee: Elected for one year at the 52nd convention, St. Louis, Mo., 1944, to fill unexpired term of Rev. R. J. Macdonald and re-elected at the 53rd, Columbus, Ohio, 1945, for a term of three years. Re-elected at the 59th, Indianapolis, Ind., 1951. Re-elected at the 62nd, Buffalo, N. Y., 1954.

ARTHUR A. MYERS
Lily Dale, N. Y.

Trustee: Elected at the 54th convention, Seattle, Wash., 1946, for a term of three years. Re-elected at the 57th, San Antonio, Texas, 1949; re-elected at the 60th, Tulsa, Okla., 1952.

PETER EVERT
Fenton, Mich.

Trustee: Elected at the 54th convention Seattle, Wash., 1946. Re-elected at the 57th, San Antonio, Texas.

JOHN H. CUDDY
Tulsa, Okla.

Trustee: Elected for a term of three years at the 60th convention, Tulsa, Okla., 1952.

NOTE: The twenty-sixth annual convention of 1918, which was called to meet at St. Louis, Mo., was not held.

Owing to an epidemic of influenza in the city, schools and churches were closed and all public meetings were forbidden.

As there could be no convention held, the officers and trustees held office until the following annual convention.

Declaration of Principles

Adopted by the
National Spiritualist Association of Churches

Sec. 1-6, Chicago, Ill., October, 1899

Sec. 7-8, Rochester, October, 1909

Sec. 9, St. Louis, Mo., October, 1944

1. We believe in Infinite Intelligence.

2. We believe that the phenomena of nature, both physical and spiritual, are the expression of Infinite Intelligence.

3. We affirm that a correct understanding of such expression and living in accordance therewith constitute true religion.

4. We affirm that the existence and personal identity of the individual continue after the change called death.

5. We affirm that communication with the so-called dead is a fact, scientifically proven by the phenomena of Spiritualism.

6. We believe that the highest morality is contained in the Golden Rule: "Whatsoever ye would that others should do unto you, do ye also unto them."

7. We affirm the moral responsibility of the individual and that he makes his own happiness or unhappiness as he obeys or disobeys Nature's physical and spiritual laws.

8. We affirm that the doorway to reformation is never closed against any human soul here or hereafter.

9. We affirm that the Precepts of Prophecy contained in the Bible are a divine attribute proven through Mediumship.

INTERPRETATION

Declaration of Principles

By JOSEPH P. WHITWELL

1. By this we express our belief in a supreme Impersonal Power, everywhere present, manifesting as life, through all forms of organized matter, called by some, God, by others, Spirit and by Spiritualists, Infinite Intelligence.

2. In this manner we express our belief in the immanence of Spirit and that all forms of life are manifestations of Spirit or Infinite Intelligence, and thus that all men are children of God.

3. A correct understanding of the laws of nature on the physical, mental and spiritual planes of life and living in accordance therewith will unfold the highest aspirations and attributes of the Soul, which is the correct function of True Religion.

4. "Life here and life hereafter is all one life whose continuity of consciousness is unbroken by that mere change in form whose process we call death." Lilian Whiting.

5. Spirit communication has been in evidence in all ages of the world and is amply recorded in both sacred and profane literature of all ages. Orthodoxy has accepted these manifestations and has interpreted them in dogma and creed in terms of the supernatural. Spiritualism accepts and recognizes these manifestations and interprets them in the understanding and light of Natural Law.

6. This precept we believe to be true. It points the way to harmony, peace and happiness. Wherever tried it has proven successful and when fully understood and practiced, will bring peace and happiness to man on earth.

7. Man himself is responsible for the welfare of the world in which he lives; for its welfare or its misery, for its happiness or unhappiness and if he is to obtain Heaven upon Earth, he must learn to make that heaven, for himself and for others. Individually, man is responsible for his own spiritual growth and welfare. Sins and wrong-doing must be outgrown and overcome. Virtue and love

INTERPRETATIONS, continued

of good must take their place. Spiritual growth and advancement must be attained by aspiration and personal striving. Vicarious atonement has no place in the philosophy of Spiritualism. Each one must carry his own cross to Calvary's Heights in the overcoming of wrong-doing and replacing them with the right.

8. We discard entirely the terrible wrong and illogical teachings of eternal damnation and in place thereof we accept and present for consideration of thinking people the thought of the continuity of life beyond the change called death.

A natural life, where the opportunity for growth and progress to better, higher and more spiritual conditions are open to all, even as they are here on the earth plane of life. We accept no such teaching as a "Hell Fire," but we do teach that sin and wrong-doing will necessarily bring remorse and suffering that would be difficult to describe in words and which can only be relieved by the individual's own efforts if not here, then in the hereafter. If we make our own lives better while here and that of our neighbors happier we shall unfold that happiness or heaven on earth which we shall carry with us into the Spirit World.

9. We thus affirm our belief in and acceptance of the truths which are contained in the Bible and assert that Prophecy and Mediumship are not unique nor of recent occurrence alone, but they are universal, everlasting and have been witnessed and observed in all ages of the world.

Definitions

Adopted by the
National Spiritualist Association of Churches

October 9—1914, October 24—1919, October 24—1951

1. Spiritualism is the Science, Philosophy and Religion of continuous life, based upon the demonstrated fact of communication, by means of mediumship, with those who live in the Spirit World.

2. A Spiritualist is one who believes, as the basis of his or her religion, in the communication between this and the spirit world by means of mediumship and who endeavors to mould his or her character and conduct in accordance with the highest teachings derived from such communication.

3. A Medium is one whose organism is sensitive to vibrations from the spirit world and through whose instrumentality, intelligences in that world are able to convey messages and produce the phenomena of Spiritualism.

4. A Spiritualist healer is one who, either through his own inherent powers or through his mediumship, is able to impart vital, curative force to pathologic conditions.

5. The Phenomena of Spiritualism consists of Prophecy, Clairvoyance, Clairaudience, Gift of Tongues, Laying on of Hands, Healing, Visions, Trance, Apports, Levitation, Raps, Automatic and Independant Writings and Paintings, Voice, Materialization, Photography, Psychometry and any other manifestation proving the continuity of life as demonstrated through the Physical and Spiritual senses and faculties of man.

"Spiritualism Is a Science" because it investigates, analyzes and classifies facts and manifestations demonstrated from the spirit side of life.

"Spiritualism Is a Philosophy" because it studies the laws of nature both on the seen and unseen sides of life and bases its conclusions upon present observed facts. It accepts statements of observed facts of past ages and conclusions drawn therefrom, when sustained by reason and by results of observed facts of the present day.

"Spiritualism Is a Religion" because it strives to understand and to comply with the Physical, Mental and Spiritual Laws of Nature, "which are the laws of God."

What Spiritualism Is and Does

It teaches personal responsibility.

It removes all fear of death, which is really the portal of the spirit world.

It teaches that death is not the cessation of life, but mere change of condition.

It teaches, not that a man has a soul, but that man is a soul and has a body.

That man is a spiritual being now, even while encased in flesh.

That as man sows on earth he reaps in the life to come.

That those who have passed on are conscious—not asleep.

That communion between the living and the "dead" is scientifically proved.

It thus brings comfort to the bereaved, and alleviates sorrow.

Spiritualism is the Science, Philosophy and Religion of continuous life, based upon the demonstrated fact of communication, by means of mediumship, with those who live in the Spirit World.

It brings to the surface man's spiritual gifts, such as inspiration, clairvoyance, clairaudience and healing powers.

It teaches that the spark of divinity dwells in all.

That as a flower gradually unfolds in beauty, so the spirit of man unfolds and develops in the spirit spheres.

Spiritualism is God's message to mortals, declaring that There Is No Death. That all who have passed on still live. That there is hope in the life beyond for the most sinful.

That every soul will progress through the ages to heights, sublime and glorious, where God Is Love and Love Is God.

It is a manifestation, a demonstration and a proof of the continuity of life and of the truth of the many Spirit manifestations recorded in the Christian Bible.

It demonstrates the many spiritual gifts with which mankind is endowed but which through want of knowledge have been allowed to lie dormant, or through prejudice have been violently and unjustly suppressed.

Objects

The object of the organized movement of Spiritualism as represented by the National Spiritualist Association of Churches may be stated in part as follows:

To teach the truths and principles expressed in the Declaration of Principles and in the Definitions of "SPIRITUALISM," "A SPIRITUALIST," "A MEDIUM" and "A SPIRITUALIST HEALER," as adopted by the National Spiritualist Association of Churches of the United States of America,

To teach and proclaim the science, philosophy and religion of modern Spiritualism, to encourage lectures on all subjects pertaining to the spiritual and secular welfare of mankind. To protest against every attempt to compel mankind to worship God in any particular or prescribed manner. To advocate and promote spiritual healing and to protect and encourage spiritual teachers and mediums in all laudable efforts in giving evidence or proof to mankind of a continued intercourse and relationship between the living and the so-called dead. To encourage every person in holding present beliefs always open to re-statement as growing thought and investigation reveal new truth, thereby leaving every individual free to follow the dictates of reason and conscience in spiritual as in secular affairs.

Naturalness of Mediumship

From the earliest revelations of man that have come down to us, writers have been bold in ascribing their talk and interviews with spirits, angels and God. They seem to distinguish between good and bad spirits and place the angels on a somewhat higher plane than that of the spirits. May it not be possible that these writers, with the unfoldment which had come to them, mistook their clairvoyant visions of exalted spirits that had progressed for angels—even for God? May it not be that those so-called inspired writers were, in reality, what today we would call advanced mediums who dedicate their psychic gifts to truth? When passive, mediums have waited for some spirit from the spirit realm to reach their consciousness and over and over again other spirits than those expected have entered their aura, claiming to be this or that one and given messages of strange and confusing nature. Well-developed mediums who cling close to truth learn how to prevent these spirits from controlling or confusing them by directly asking aid from the guides whom they have learned are worthy of absolute trust. Unfortunately, there are many mediums who, in a trance state, open wide their door for any spirit to enter. Such mediums bring to the sitter often the strangest and most unintelligible messages. I have sometimes felt that those undeveloped, undisciplined mediums were the sport of the lower spirits who had ascended from mortals passed from the earth plane before they had learned anything of the depth and beauty of meaning reflected from the lives of those representing progressive humanity.

Floyd B. Wilson in *"Man Limitless."*

Philosophy of Spiritualism

(In Brief)

Infinite Intelligence

Infinite Intelligence pervades and controls the universe, is without shape or form and is impersonal, omnipresent and omnipotent.

The Universe: Its Origin and Government

The origin of the universe, for all practical purposes, may be said to be unknown and without special bearing on moral conduct. The universe is an aggregation of forces and matter, which always moves and acts in the same manner under the same conditions and is not capriciously governed.

The Evolution of Man

Man is a spiritual being, evolved from the lower forms of life, up through the period of consciousness, to the state of the higher moral and spiritual faculties, which survive, unaffected, the decomposition of the physical body.

Man's Duty on Earth

The whole duty of man in his mortal life consists in taking the first steps in the attainment of knowledge and in gradually developing his character and nature to harmonize with the fully unfolded spiritual state. This duty compasses the entire conduct of man, mentally, morally and spiritually.

Brotherhood of Man

By virtue of similar qualities, conditions, wants and aspirations, mankind is a brotherhood; and in this life, at least, cannot escape the good or evil effects of contact and conversation. It is, therefore, necessary that this brotherhood be promoted by the more fortunate ones for the betterment and upliftment of the less fortunate.

Man's Individuality

In the spirit world man retains his individuality and the unfoldment of his mental, moral and spiritual faculties is continued indefinitely by processes not unlike the manner pertaining to this world.

Matter and Spirit Always Co-related

As matter and spirit are in conjunction in man, so are they found co-related throughout the universe. Spirit is able to manifest only through substance.

Music and Harmony

Harmony, or the Music of the Spheres, as it is sometimes called is the direct result of Spirit in definite harmonious action.

The planes of action seem to be arranged and expressed, much as the octaves on the musical key board.

Between certain points of rhythm we get certain quality of tone in all its variations.

Starting with the octave, based on natural C, the octave above or below produces the quality of tone that is expresssed in the rhythm of its higher or lower pitch and thus produces its own tone, not out of harmony with the first, but when rightly placed, blending in perfect harmony with the first.

So the plane of life, referred to as Spirit Life, or Spirit World, is an expression of life and power, manifesting under perfectly natural laws, in a higher sphere or rhythm of expression than that of the Mortal Plane.

Mortal Life, being analogous to the octave based on natural C, we realize that the vibration of the Spirit World is the direct result of Spirit, in definite action, on a higher pitch or rhythm than that of the Mortal Plane.

There is an octave below the one we call "Mortal Life" which is known as the world of "Microscopic Life" which is as tangible and real as life in any of its manifestations. This octave is the lower pitch or rhythm.

All of these octaves melt and blend in perfect harmony for the individual who is in a high mental and spiritual attitude and condition. He is then "At One" with them all and grows conscious of each and it is then that he realizes that "All This Boundless Universe Is Life," and "There Are No Dead."

Man's Moral Status After Death

After the spirit has severed its relations with the physical body, man's moral status is the same as immediately before the change and he enters into a high or low estate according to his attainments in this world. By a subtle law both the good and the evil he has done are fairly weighed; he himself holds the scales and renders the judgment.

Earthly Deeds Affect Spiritual Existence

Good deeds, springing from a good heart, have a creative force in building pleasant abodes in spirit life, and conversely the sinful create their own unhappy habitations. The wicked must compensate for their evil deeds, here or hereafter and attain a state of justice before they are prepared to enter upon the path which leads to spiritual happiness and progression.

Spirit Manifestations

The inhabitants of the spirit world, under proper conditions, have the power to and many do, return to this world and manifest themselves in various ways, from a mental suggestion to a visual appearance. They sometimes take possession of the brain of sensitive mortals and function through them mentally and physically. The extent to which this can be done depends upon the knowledge of the controlling spirit and the kind and degree of mediumistic qualities possessed by the sensitive.

Spirit Communications to Be Tested

Communications from the spirit world are not necessarily infallible truths, but may partake of the imperfections of the mind from which they emanate and of the channels through which they come, and are, moreover, subject to misinterpretation by those to whom they are given.

No inspired communication, in this or any past age, whatever claims may be or have been set up as to its source, is authoritative beyond the truth it expresses to the person to whom it is given. Truth is the standard by which all inspired and all spiritual teachings must be tested. There were false as well as true prophets in Old Testament times, as well as in the present age.

Inspiration Perpetual

Inspiration, or the influx of ideas and promptings from the spirit world, is not a miracle of a past age, but a perpetual fact, the ceaseless method of Infinite Intelligence for human elevation.

Mediumship

Mediumship does not depend upon belief or goodness. It has been manifested in all ages, to men of all faiths, to the good, the bad and the indifferent. Goodness and character are the result of individual effort, self control and earnest desire. The truths of Spiritualism have been established after much questioning, much examination, much comparison and much testing. They have come for many years through mediums all over the globe and from many different spiritual sources, with wonderful unanimity; and they satisfy our reason and our sense of justice.

Children Grow in the Spirit World

Children and other persons passing over before they have reached their full stature, grow to the full stature in the spirit world; but they are able, by the exercise of will power, to make their appearance, in size and form, as it was at the time of their passing. These laws apply also to the babe who dies physically unborn.

Happiness Attainable by All

All dwellers in the spirit world who are willing may attain a state of complete happiness, but in cases of some evil-doers much suffering must be endured before they can free their imaginations from the scenes of their evil deeds or their souls from the sense of guilt. Spiritual happiness does not depend primarily upon belief or creed, but upon character. Salvation from the results of sin is not a gift; it must be worked out by the individual with the aid of such advice and instruction as others may give.

Purpose of Spirit Life

The purpose of life in the spirit world is to unfold the mental, moral and spiritual faculties; to study the works of nature, to help perverse and undeveloped spirits out of their low condition, to minister to earth's children, either through influence directly exerted or through the instrumentality of mediums, to enjoy the fellowship of kindred minds and to share the sweetness of pure love; in short, to complete the individualization of the human soul.

Hiding Man's Divinity

The God's, having stolen from man his divinity, met in council to discuss where they should hide it. One suggested that it be carried to the other side of the earth and buried; but it was pointed out that man is a great wanderer and that he might find the lost treasure on the other side of the earth. Another proposed that it be dropped into the depths of the sea; but the same fear was expressed—that man, in his insatiable curiosity, might dive deep enough to find it even there. Finally, after a space of silence, the oldest and wisest of the Gods said: "Hide it in man himself as that is last place he will ever think to look for it." And it was agreed, all seeing it's subtle and wise strategy.

Man wandered over the earth for ages, searching in all places, high and low, far and near, before he thought to look within himself for the divinity he sought. At last, slowly, dimly, he began to realize that what he thought was far off, hidden in "the pathos of distance" is nearer than the breath he breathes, even in his own heart.

J. F. NEWTON.

Invocation and Reading No. 1

Invocation

To the Infinite Spirit of the Universe, manifesting love and tenderness from fragile flower to mightiest oak; ever expressing Infinite care and wisdom; creating a desire for a more complete understanding of life's obligations and opportunities, we would attune ourselves, knowing that from this contact comes a more perfect understanding of the laws which govern our being, a more perfect comprehension of our duties and greater courage to face our daily tasks. We would learn more of that great spirit world to which we journey—more of its nature, its illuminations, it's glories. May we discover more and more avenues of communication between the two worlds and attain a higher, a truer, a deeper appreciation of the blessed Gospel of Spiritualism. May we continue to grow in knowledge and wisdom and through our sensitized instruments reach humanity everywhere bringing into their lives this great Truth which has brought such joy, peace and understanding into our own souls. Amen.

Reading: What Is Spiritualism?

Spiritualism is an outpouring of Spirit upon humanity, a divine revelation from the spheres of light. It is the highest message of truth which we have as yet, grown to grasp; and one whose depth, beauty and mighty significance we still imperfectly realize.

How little as yet, we know of true Spiritualism. How far we are from mastering its wonderful philosophy! It cannot be contained between the covers of any book or outlined fully in any written creed.

Spiritualism is the broad educator, the great redeemer, the emancipator which releases human souls from the bondage of superstition and ignorance, lifts the clouds of error that have so long enshrouded the world and illumines the darkness of the world's materiality.

It has given freedom to slaves and broken the shackles of mental bondage. It has introduced more enlightened methods of healing and was chief factor in the larger emancipation of woman. Through the gateway of inspired mediumship it has breathed forth poesy and melody. It has stimulated science and enriched philosophy. It has broadened the conceptions of men and liberalized beliefs and creeds.

It is the tender nurse in sorrow, the kind physician for every need, physical or spiritual, the universal comforter. It has taken away the sting of death and left to the grave no victory.

It has abundantly proved that there is no death, that there is a world of spirit and we are its denizens, here and now. Hence there can be no separation between spirit and spirit under any circumstances, clothed or unclothed with clay.

It is only physical sight that suffers loss; and gradually our eyes are being cleansed from earthly dust, to discern spiritual things and our mortal ears unstopped to catch higher vibrations than mundane atmosphere conveys.

The intuitive spirit receives supernal messages from centers of inspiration in the upper realms and grander revelations will be vouchsafed as we grow ready to receive them.

May greater receptivity be ours to gain more and more of truth and to live the truth we know. May we be not content to merely believe in spirit communication. Let us live our Spiritualism with fidelity, fearless of the unenlightened opinions of men.

Let us love truly, unselfishly. May our charity even for those who wrong us be strong and all embracing. Let our forgiveness be perfect and unexacting; our patience, serene and godlike.

May we ever increase in all spiritual knowledge. May we know by rich experience, the potentialities of spirit, and learn, while yet embodied, what it is to be a free masterful spirit capable even now, of every noble conquest and achievement.

Benediction

May the sacred impressions reaching us from realms supernal ever guide our footsteps aright in the great journey of life. Amen.

Invocation and Reading No. 2

Invocation

With perfect faith in the power of spirit, we direct our thoughts in this hour of devotion to the great Oversoul of ALL knowing that every aspiration, every holy desire, will find fruition in our lives. With simple perfect faith we come with all our yearnings and aspirations, knowing they will be answered to the degree we harmoniously attune ourselves with nature's immutable laws. May all our heartaches, all our loneliness, all our despair be conquered as we grow in spiritual understanding from day to day. Teach us, O Dwellers in the Land Supernal, to bear with patience and fortitude the burdens and vexations of fleeting time and to accept all seeming disappointments as lessons in the development of our spiritual lives. May the work of bridging the chasm of death be so sweetly performed that pain may be transformed into joy and sorrow into peace and happiness. Amen.

Reading: Power of Spirits

How great the power of spirits! A host of invisible intelligences, exalted and wise, surround us everywhere. They cause men to purify their hearts and rectify their lives. They are everywhere, beside us, around us, above us. "Millions of spiritual BEINGS walk the earth unseen, both when we wake and when we sleep."

All these with ceaseless praise, by day and by night, behold the works of Infinite Intelligence and adore them. Are they not all ministering spirits sent forth to minister to those who walk in the light and to save those who walk in darkness? Yea, the angels attend the pure in heart and surround them with a halo of light and melody.

They come to lead the weary pilgrims from the rude scenes of this life to the mansions of the blessed. They come to guide the erring one and win his heart from evil. They breathe a holy calm into the wounded heart. The glory of their presence dissipates the darkness of this world.

Who are these angel ministers? They are the wise and good of every age, of every land, who come laden with love, to bless cheer and comfort sorrowing mankind. Under their loving tuition our spiritual senses may be unfolded so that they both appear and speak to us.

O! Angels of Light and Wisdom, we solicit your presence with us this day, that you may illumine our minds, quicken our understanding, warm our hearts and strengthen our adherence to truth. May your light drive away the mists of doubt and superstition from our minds so that the light of Divine Truth may be ours forever.

Benediction

May the guidance of spirit loved ones illumine our minds, quicken our understanding and inspire us to live in accord with the dictates of truth. Amen.

Invocation and Reading No. 3

Invocation

O Great Infinite Intelligence, creative power of the Universe which gives to every form of life in nature's temple a voice of praise —to the songbirds in the trees, to the great deep that ceaselessly rolls its anthem and to the worlds that speed onward through limitless space. While we share in the joyfulness of the ever-living winds and waves, we know that in that higher temple, the temple of the soul there are voices that ever speak aloud for truth, for justice and for liberty. We are indeed grateful to know that the soul of man is immortal and that the Universe with all its sublimity, is the soul's eternal heritage. We are happy for the knowledge of the higher and diviner life, which even now stamps the living clay with the images of immortal thought and beauty. May the light of immortality which streams in and through the illuminated chambers of the human brain dispel the shadows of doubt and fear and terror of death. May the Star of Knowledge never fade, the Moon of Wisdom never be eclipsed and may the Sun of Spiritual Power eternally replenish its resplendent light. Amen.

Life's Anchor

Rise, O Soul, to higher things! Be exalted in the light of thine own radiance and strength!

How vast, how limitless are the resources of the Soul!
How unexplored the deep repository of eternal attributes!
How skillfully hidden from mortal view!

Beneath the strength and skill of the physical body, beneath the achievements and unrest of mortal mind lies the unperturbed soul of man, like the calm waters of the sea beneath the surging waves. Beneath the ever-changing mortal part of man lies the soul like an impenetrable rock beneath the shifting sands, anchoring man to earth until the experiences of this terrestrial plane have prepared him for celestial existence.

What is the rock that securely anchors man to earth life? What is beneath the physical and mental self that manifests automatically the attributes of the Eternal? Underlying all is a reality which has ever indicated man is not annihilated when the physical body loses

INVOCATION AND READING No. 3

its animation. Throughout the ages man's desire to prove this observation has developed religion. Man's firm conviction that an eternal something exists back of and beneath all life is a nearly universal belief.

What is man's relation to this reality?
How may man come in contact with its attributes?
Is there a spiritual key to unlock its mysteries?
"SEEK AND YE SHALL FIND."

Ye shall find Power—limitless and available. Widom—to conciliate and reassure. Goodness—the result of conquering the lower self. Hope—the hope of immortality. Faith—the comfort that dispels all doubt. Peace—the calmness born of trust and understanding. Light—the revealer of Truth and Love—the dispeller of spiritual darkness, the reflector of the Divine in the Universe. Thus, the underneath stands revealed. From the plan and purpose of these spiritual attributes Infinite Intelligence weaves the threads of Life draping mortals in garments of their own divinity.

But the Soul—the glittering rock of Eternal Truth is ever beneath the turbulent waters holding man securely, radiating peace, a soft music that makes his every step in life a benediction; wisdom, creating awareness from the experiences acquired in the immeasurable yesterdays and love guiding all in paths of service.

Led by wisdom's light, guarded by loved ones in Spirit, man continues the journey of life, knowing that "through the qualities of the soul all shall arrive."

That instinct for life, for immortality will not die. Life is written on the ascending scale. All are guided by the soul's conviction.

There is no death—Our souls shall rise as our Guiding Star.
Call aloud, O Soul, proclaim this Truth unto all the earth!

Benediction

May the beacon light of truth flash its rays on our pathway through life, bringing peace, hope and joy into the lives of all. Amen.

Invocation and Reading No. 4

Invocation

We lift our hearts to the Great Oversoul which ever expresses through this still small voice within, in our desire to be more sensitive to the vibrations of that great world of Spirit. Give us something of the patience of the old oak trees in our endeavors to grow in understanding of basic truth, something of the simplicity of the flowers, in our faith and acceptance of spirit guidance. Give us somewhat of that wonderful power that sweeps the earth in storm and wind; something of the steadiness of the stars that nightly shine and the sun that wanes not. No common care would we neglect, but with faithful performance sanctify every deed and act. So we ask that the wise spirits, who are ever ready to guide and to help even the weakest child of earth, may draw near to us and teach us the way to everlasting peace. Amen.

Reading: Self-Reliance

Trust thyself: The man with greatness of soul is he who in the midst of the crowd keeps with perfect composure the independence of solitude, who under the weight of great misfortunes keeps a serene and equal mind.

If we live truly, we shall see truly and our intellectual and emotional faculties will be more accurately attuned to nature. Let us be strong and refuse to be weak; let us think for ourselves and not be overawed by so-called ancient authority.

When the mind in its revived vigor takes hold of new conceptions, we shall gladly unburden the memory of its hoarded load of misconceived doctrines.

When a man lives with the Divine, the grosser concepts gradually fall away from him, his mental horizon becomes clarified, his heart becomes more tender, his voice becomes as sweet as the murmur of the brook and the rustle of the corn, but his resolution becomes firmer and his courage dauntless.

Insist on thyself; do not imitate; yet imitation is better than stagnation. Thine own gift thou canst present every moment with the cumulative force of a whole nation's cultivation; but of the adopted talent of another thou hast only a temporary half-possession.

INVOCATION AND READING No. 4

That which each can do best none but Nature can teach him. Do that which is justly assigned to thee, be it great or small, for thou canst not hope too much or dare too much, nor canst thou be abased by faithfully performing small duties.

The patriarchs have delivered words of wisdom for the benefit of those who aspire for and seek inspiration:

"Each man to himself and each woman to herself is the word of the past and present and the true word on immortality."

"No one can acquire for another—not one; no one can grow for another—not one."

"No man is ever poor who looks for what he wants within himself."

"Behold a part of Divinity itself within thee: remember thine own dignity, nor dare to descend to evil or to meanness."

"Respect thine own nature; but to do this, thou must have things within thee to respect."

"To thine own self be true and it must follow, as the night the day, thou canst not then be false to any man."

Thus have great minds impressed upon us man's capacity for using divine powers. How the thought of the dignity, the nobility and the spiritual potency of man lifts us from the dust! With this thought held firmly in mind no man can occupy a servile position in the world—no man can be a slave.

Being aware of the inherent powers of the soul, man must ever seek to make them dominant in the outward life. To do this, he must be ever true to the inward light which maketh all things plain and shines for the guidance of all the nations.

Benediction

May the presence of your spirit loved ones ever envelop you with spiritual power, protecting and guiding you always. Amen.

Invocation and Reading No. 5

Invocation

O Spirit of Infinite Wisdom and Love, we yearn to come into a more perfect understanding of things spiritual. We aspire to express more of the beauty of the higher life: that sweet spiritual life which breathes upon a world weary and heavy-laden with heartaches and pains. With this deep purpose, this lofty ideal always before us, there is no yearning for former pleasures, no desire to seek the material conditions of life; but always a desire to strive for the purer and nobler things of the intellect and soul. We earnestly pray that we may always see the blessing shining through every dark and painful condition. When in our service to our fellow man, we become weary and downhearted, may the spirit messengers of light and love bring us comfort relief and encouragement. May we join forces with those ministering angels bringing consolation to the downcast, happiness to the sad, love to the friendless and hope to the despairing. Amen.

Reading: Death, the Gateway to Life.

Let us consider the mission of Death. Millions through the ages have beheld death with terror. Let us dispel the gloom. O death, thou givest a broader liberty, a more glorious freedom to the soul.

The door of thy castle swings inward, noiselessly opening upon enchanted chambers, radiant with unwonted light and glory, such as earth hath never known.

Thou kisseth down the eyelids in sleep, O death and dost imprint upon the lips the seal of immortality. Beautiful indeed at thy gentle touch hath been the awakening into new experiences.

Not into a new life but into a new individual experience, for it is the same life that has unfalteringly kept its march through the ages and thou bringst its fuller realization.

New fields, O human Soul, lie open before thee; loftier heights than ever thy feet have scaled stretch up and on before thee.

Death hath not robbed thee of thy treasures. All the good thou hast done, all the noble thoughts thou hast expressed, live and are with thee still. O death, thou holdst within thy hands the key which unlocks the door of space and time.

INVOCATION AND READING No. 5

Art thou bereft of friends and loved ones? Doth sorrow rest heavily upon thy aching head? and doth thy tired spirit seek for rest? Thou are not alone; thy friends and loved ones were never so near to thee as now. All fetters broken, thy friends can draw nearer to thee now than ever before.

The sweet communion of spirit with spirit shall cool thy fevered aching brow, and assuage thy lurking sorrow. Thy heart bowed down shall beat again with lightness and with ecstasy.

Rest shall thou find O Soul in the midst of thy sorrow, and thou shalt hold divinest communion with kindred spirits. What more exalting and uplifting than the communion and fellowship of emancipated spirits! In silence, soul speaks to soul; thought leaps forth without sound; intelligence is transmitted upon gentle waves of ether.

Then hast thou O Soul, realized thy relationship with Eternal Spirit. The spirit of man is indestructible, his soul immortal, his individuality everlasting, therefore let us not mourn and lament over Death—for Death is the gateway of life.

Benediction

May the understanding of our minds, the meditation of our hearts and the obedience of our will to the still small voice within, lead us to live our Spiritualism with fidelity and fearlessness. Amen.

Invocation and Reading No. 6

Invocation

O Spirit of Infinite Love and Tenderness, we lift our hearts in grateful assurance that in answer to our aspirations, strong and wise and lofty spirits will come to guide direct and guard us. The yearnings of our hearts to do, to work, to serve, must ever be of some service in the world. The desire to create something of happiness and peace and joy in the troubled hearts of those who suffer, must ever find its answer in a better life, a better order in the community, a more spiritualized people. Though sometimes the shadows fall across our pathway and the light is shut away from us and we see only dimly the steps we are to take, yet we know spirit power is guiding us, that the love of our spirit people is supporting and sustaining us. Wherever there is a heart that aches, wherever shadow brings tears of sadness or distress, there may we go, and with this truth of the tender love and ministering spirits bring understanding, love and joy. Amen.

Reading: True Religion

True religion leads us to live better and truer lives.

It makes us observe a stricter honesty in all our dealings with mankind.

It causes us to search our own hearts and make them clean and pure—free from all taint of selfishness—free from everything that can debase.

It implants within us principles and motives which help us to withstand all the evil temptations which beset the pathway of life.

Gautama Buddha said: "One's own self it is indeed difficult to subdue." A voice from the spirit has told us that virtue is the exercise of sufficient will power to avoid that which is hurtful.

Progress in personal morality is possible for every human being and to aid in this progress is the aim of all true religion.

There is a commandment which echoes through every human breast, saying:

"Be thou perfect; conform thy life to high standards. Man is his own savior, and the soul that can render an honest and aspiring life commands all light, all influence, all fate."

INVOCATION AND READING No. 6

Let us labor until there shall be a grand unison of efforts toward a common goal, whose achievement shall uplift the race, whose coming shall send gladness to the hearts of those who are weary and heavy-laden.

Work is an element in developing our spirits, when done with fidelity and purity of purpose; therefore, work enters into the results of all true religion. Yea, work is a joy, both for the doer and the person for whom it is done, when it is consecrated by brotherly-love.

Such work bears an invisible flower and fruit—the flower and fruit of character, of real accomplishment, of true religion. True religion encourages men to mutual helpfulness, to generosity and to kindliness in word and deed.

Under its influence we are led to stretch a helpful hand to those who are bruised or broken—to make sorrow more endurable and temptations easier to conquer, to make the losses lighter and to lift the sense of shame from the sinful soul.

Then may we exclaim with the poet:
"Through love to light! Oh, wonderful the way
That leads from darkness to perfect day;
From darkness and from dolor of the night
To morning that comes singing o'er the sea!
Through love to light! Through light, O God, to thee,
Who art the Love of love, the Eternal Light of light!"

Benediction

May the light of truth shine in your lives and the potentialities of spirit unfold, that you may realize through your inner consciousness, your at-one-ment with Infinite Intelligence. Amen.

Invocation and Reading No. 7

Invocation

O Spirit of Infinite Love and Tenderness, we lift our hearts in praise and joy and thanksgiving for the blessed opportunity of opening the door of that other life that our beloved in spirit may come through to give us wisdom, strength and understanding. So vast is this wonderful opportunity, so far extending in its power and its beauty, that we cannot at once come into the full realization of it. This much we do know, that love finds its own and speaks out of its heart all of the experiences that may benefit humanity. Like children groping through the darkness and seeking for the loved hand, listening for the voice that is dearer and sweeter than all the music in the world, we come today and listen again, not only for our own, but perchance to catch the message from someone who yearns to find the old home and the old associations. The sweetest expression for spiritual life is service, so we offer ourselves for the service of the spirit world. May they find us ready. May they find no wilfulness, no inharmony, nothing which shall impede their free and full expression. Bless us in our undertaking, help us to grow in wisdom. Amen.

Reading: Divinity of Nature

Nature's demands are the only true guides to usefulness, probity and progression. To know these demands is all we need to know; faithfully to comply with them is all we need to do, if we would become all we are designed to be and all we are capable of being. He who most perfectly understands the demands of Nature, in regard to his own and his neighbor's body and soul, most perfectly understands the operations of that Infinite Intelligence which manifests itself in all nature.

He walks in the light and lives in the right, who seeks the truth in Nature's book and moulds his life accordingly. We and our neighbors are parts of Nature, therefore, what we do to our neighbors, we do to ourselves. Every act reflects upon ourselves.

Let this be the one controlling thought in our treatment of the men, women and children around us. Every indignity shown to our neighbor is an indignity to ourselves; every insult or wrong done man, woman or child, of whatever country, color or condition, is done to ourselves.

What we feel toward our neighbor, is a measure of our nobility or littleness of soul. To love our neighbor, is to love the divinity in man. Those whose loving and tender reverence for their fellow-kind is so profound as to make them prefer to die rather than to injure the least of them, are the only ones who really perceive the grandeur of the divine life.

Let us inspire our neighbors, by our actions, with an idea of the divinity of human nature. Let us purify the magnetic atmosphere in which we move and dwell, that it may be radiant with health-giving forces.

Let us be reverent, so that sweet peace may come into our souls like the rosy morning light into the bosom of the opening blossom. Let our hearts and souls be clean pure sweet temples fit for the divine to dwell therein. Let each one of us obey his deepest, highest and purest promptings.

The glory is his, who has been noble and mighty in word and work, who has felt the truth and even at the price of his own blood has sought to make it triumph. In his soul shall be outwrought every demand of divine Nature. In the spiritualization of mankind, Nature's divine harmonies are perfected.

We are all architects, builders and decorators and our work is beautiful or unsightly, as we obey or disobey Nature's divine demands. He who simply indulges in carnal ease and pleasure, is in danger of losing his highest self for a long and painful night, among the dark and heavy shadows.

He who is ever faithful to his best ideals, through changes and fatigue, through opposition and injury, shall reach the loftiest spiritual heights and hold communion with saints and sages.

Benediction

May the philosophy of the continuity of life and the communication of spirit enlarge your spiritual horizon, bringing into view your sacred duty to self and to all mankind—to love and serve one another. Amen.

Invocation and Reading No. 8

Invocation

Again the day dawns; again the sun is shining; and the songbirds sing and all the world is awake with gladness and joy. Only the hearts of those who do not feel the glory of living, the joy of life, the peace of progress, are sad and unhappy. Help us, O Angel Loved Ones, to rise above the doubts, the fears, the pains and the anguish of this life, that we may be fitting instruments to carry the word of assurance, of knowledge, of love, to all who are in the shadows and have not yet found comfort for their souls and who are ignorant of the fact of spirit communication. The knowledge of this communication is the golden thread which glorifies and sanctifies and beautifies whatever of the sombre shade may work itself into the fabric of life. Open our natures to great revelations; give us eyes to see, ears to hear, and hands to do; that we may work with greater efficiency and zeal for those who labor with little hope of reward in this life and vision no life beyond the portals of the tomb. Bless us in our effort to bring to the attention of humanity the gospel of the continuity of life. Give us patience in the work and keep our hearts ever understanding and sympathetic. Amen.

Reading: Road to Happiness

Would you be happy while you dwell on earth? If so pull up the thorn trees from the garden of your life and plant in place thereof the myrtle trees of affection. Then will your days be filled with sunshine and your paths be paths of peace.

Would you be a daily blessing to your neighbors? If so, cast upon the vibrating ether tender thoughts of loving kindness daily, for they shall find lodgment in some heart.

Do you long for opportunities to become good and great? If so, conquer self, master the unruly passions, cultivate the intellect and apply your powers for humanity's good.

Are you in love with life? If so, "know thyself," for in so doing you shall learn the laws which expand and prolong life and you shall perceive the nobility of giving no unnecessary pain to any living creature.

Do you seek knowledge? If so despise not the small things;

deem nothing too sacred for honest investigation; sound the reasons for things, meditate upon the wisdom of the learned, but accept only Truth as a final authority.

Are you in sorrow and in need of consolation? If so, go forth on some errand of mercy; minister unto the sorrowing; speak words of comfort to the distressed and the despairing, for thus shall you find what you impart to others.

Are you distressed with thoughts of the wrongs done? If so, resolve to do wrong no more; open the windows of your soul and let the sunshine in; seek the companionship of the good, ask for the aid of invisible helpers and set yourself some worthy task.

Are you satisfied with self? If so, learn from the truly great and good how small are your attainments, how crude your development; look into the starry heavens and learn to be humble; seek to answer the questions of a child and learn the limitations of your wisdom.

Benediction

May the knowledge and proof of spirit communication make Life more understandable and Death, our friend. Amen.

Invocation and Reading No. 9

Invocation

Through meditation in the depths of silence, we would rise to greater wisdom and spirituality. Into the vast universe of truth we would send our spirits to be bathed in the purifying currents of love, that we may live the life for which we yearn and toward which our souls aspire. We would be made strong by the inflowing of Infinite Love; we would patiently endure whatever falls to our lot, knowing that the path of rectitude leads up and out to glorious beauty, freedom and light. We would not selfishly strive to achieve, nor shirk the labor fraught with pain and suffering. With the strong arms of faith and tenderness, we would hold all the souls that reach out to us for help or strength. Though we sometimes may be weary and discouraged, yet through every wearisome and discouraging hour the bright light of knowledge shines and makes the way clear. We are thankful for the renewed spiritual power which comes to us when we enter the silence to hold communion with the spirit world. We pray that we may be instrumental in bringing many others to a realization of this great truth, that we may bring peace to the troubled heart and comfort to the suffering soul. May every word that is here spoken be filled with devotion. May harmony prevail and may we all feel that it is good to be here. Amen.

Reading: Into the Silence

In the silence would I walk with thee. There would I adorn my thoughts with noble ideals. There would I develop and strengthen my character. In this silence geniuses are born. Out of the infinite depth of silence proceeds all that is. In the silence awe and reverence abide with me, the great wave of truth envelops me and purifies my soul, urging me to scale the heights, and be glorified by the light that glows and plays forever above their summits.

What power there is in silence: there, resolutions are formed, sublime conquests effected. Here the soul secretly feels the power of Infinite Intelligence and emerges strengthened. In the silence commune with thyself; find there thy mission in the world. There let the message come to thee that thou shalt give unto those who have become seekers after the light. In the silence find the glowing pathway of the spirit. Humble though thy work may be, lowly thy mission in the world, thou shalt learn its meaning, and thou shalt be contented to labor and to wait. Thy soul shall be blessed with the rich increase of celestial knowledge, all perplexities shall vanish, all troubles shall cease, all sorrow be assuaged. The clouds shall lift and ineffable light encompass thee. Thy soul shall find its own and commune with the loved ones in the voiceless language of the soul. From the silence thou shalt return, seeking no longer far and wide thy mission in the world, for thy message in glowing, burning eloquence speaks in every act. Obey the voice that speaks when all other voices are silent and all will be well with thee.

In the silence, I lift my thoughts to the angels, yea, even unto the Infinite, pleading for food such as earth giveth not. I thirst for the great draughts of light that flood the upper heavens and I hunger for the inspiration of great and noble minds. Beneath all is dark, above all is light, then be lifted up to realms celestial. Let calmness and peace steal over thee that the world is unable to give or take away.

Benediction

May normalcy of health, peace of mind and calmness of spirit attune you with the Infinite that all may be well with thee. Amen.

Invocation and Reading No. 10

Invocation

O Eternal and Everlasting Spirit of the Universe, we would reverently take up the duties of life; we would pursue our way along the path which leads through the busy haunts of men, to take by the hand those who have struggled, who are yearning, who are weeping and frightened; we would give them the light which has come to us through the ministrations of loving spirits; we would whisper to them words of cheer and encouragement and give them a glimpse of the spiritual heights and of the life beautiful. We would lead men to a better understanding of the great forces of life and of the wonderful opportunities that await the spirit in the life hereafter. O Divine Spirit, give us a truer appreciation of the nobility and grandeur of struggling upward, onward and forward. May spirit loved ones help us in every effort to improve ourselves and encourage us in our endeavors to uplift our fellowmen and make their lives sweeter and brighter. Amen.

Reading—Inspiration

Believe in self. Know you are a god in embryo! This is the sublimest and most comforting fact in the world, giving assurance of man's individualized eternal existence. Man is a conscious entity; in consciousness lies character. Eternal life begins when man begins to live his divinity, the higher side of his character.

When man has risen to the height where he recognizes the divine in the world in himself and in his fellowman, he realizes his own immortality and yearns to express that love which is within.

It is the same love that permeates us with reverent faith and tender affection for our departed which brings back the hosts of men, women and children from the higher life.

Hearts are dust, but hearts' loves are eternal and inspire man to greater spiritual light, for the attainment of his ideals. In his efforts he pronounces his own eulogy in the influence he exercises as it affects the lives of his fellows.

In aspiring, man increases his knowledge, widens his horizon of understanding, deepens his thought, attains a culture of conscience and the apprehension of his eternal existence. Aspiration precedes inspiration. Through it man attains a self-development that lifts him to a higher and nobler conception of life's duties and privileges. He develops reason and judgment, qualities that are never instantaneous.

Man receives inspiration from the achievements of the great, past and present, realizing all comes from Spirit. If man heeds the promptings of Spirit, his life may be an inspiration to others. He is inspired only in ratio as he hears and obeys that still small voice within. Inspiration reaches man consistent with his fitness and capacity to receive. Aspire to be a fit receptacle! Set an ideal! Aspire! and inspiration will bring great and enduring accomplishments.

There are no dull moments for an inspired mind. Life is rich and productive in proportion as one begins each day with right intent and applies himself with sincerity and diligence to the task before him, determining his degree of success and happiness.

What inspiration is keener that Spiritualism? When man realizes his departed loved ones are ever within sight, sound and touch, trying to impress him, surely this fact inspires him to be a better person and aspire to higher ideals.

Heed the impressions from the Spirit World—hear and respond, do not ignore. Be inspired through Nature's lessons in this world. Realize all we have do or are, are the expression of some inspiration. Holy Writ teems with it, proving it a plural process. When a Voice from the Beyond spoke to the prophets of old—it spoke through them to *all people*. Likewise: Pass the joy and knowledge *you* receive on to others. Remember! SOMEBODY is waiting for your inspiration.

Benediction

May the blessings of the Spirit World be showered upon you like the rains of Spring, fertilizing the spiritual seed planted in your minds tonight, bringing forth a harvest of spiritual good that you may go forth in a more sincere, earnest endeavor to obtain more and greater knowledge regarding life here and hereafter. Amen.

Invocation and Reading No. 11

Invocation

O Infinite Spirit of Wisdom and Love permeating this entire universe with greatness immeasurably beyond the grasp of finite minds, reveal to us avenues through which we can better seek the true and the beautiful; and, through which we may be enabled to gain in knowledge and strength to overcome our weakness—spiritual, moral, mental or physical; and, through which we may attain happiness and come closer en rapport with the spirit world. Grant us courage and wisdom to do our duty at all times; to endure with patience the trials that beset our path; to aid others wisely and effectively; impress us to have charity and compassion for those who are weaker than ourselves; give us strength to resist temptation; bless us through the knowledge of the presence and the help of ethereal visitors, that we may fit ourselves for the company of the pure and upright, here and hereafter. Amen.

Reading: Wisdom and Love

Love and Wisdom are the handmaidens of Divinity; they give strength and righteousness to character and right direction to action and thought. To know one's self is wisdom; and to judge justly, to think purely, and to act charitably are the fruits of wisdom.

The lips of the wise man dispense knowledge; but the heart of the foolish breeds confusion. Through experience and knowledge, wisdom cometh to him who seeks to harmonize his life with Nature's divine order.

Wisdom is one of the principal things; therefore, get wisdom; for in getting wisdom thou shalt surely get understanding. Happy is the man who getteth wisdom and hath understanding, for he shall stand before the great and mighty, calm and dauntless.

The possession of wisdom is of greater value than much silver or fine gold; and more to be desired than empty honor, fleeting place and fickle favor. Wisdom is more precious than rubies; and all the wordly things thou canst desire are not to be compared with her.

"Her ways are ways of pleasantness and all her paths are peace." She giveth length of days and a quiet breast to those who hold and retain her teaching. Wisdom is a shining lamp to him who holds fast to her along life's stony road.

Wisdom is a grateful remedy for the biting ills of life; it is a strong lever wherewith we may lift the heavy weight of sorrow from the soul. Wisdom is the bridge which spans the wild stream of ignorance and carries us safely over the stormy waters of passion.

Across life's sea to the haven of death, Wisdom is the strong bark which weathers wind and wave.

Be humble, if thou wouldst attain to wisdom, for it abideth not in the bosom of the proud and self-satisfied. Trim the lamp of wisdom; let its rays shine into the dark corners of the world, to guide the feet of the erring ones and to give hope to those whose spirits are dark with error. Wisdom united with love giveth the spirit great strength to achieve and to endure.

To love is to expand the affections; it is the death of selfishness. Love removeth all unkindness, therefore, love one another. Love floweth from a sweet and wholesome fountain, and blessed are they who quench their thirst thereat.

Love hath prophetic eyes; it seeeth the triumph of good in the darkest hour; it forsaketh never, but findeth its own and keepeth it safe.

Love is the fulfilling of the law. Love is the greatest thing in the world. Love is the greatest thing in the universe. "God is Love."

Benediction

May effort, wisely directed, bring into your consciousness the proof of everlasting life, the joy of spirit communication and the knowledge of life in active progressive realms beyond the plane of mortality. Amen.

Invocation and Reading No. 12

Easter

Invocation

O Great Guiding Force from out the Land of Spirit!—may we in our privileged hour of communing in sacred fellowship, be worthy of its true import and radiance, be captives of the impressions and impulses coming from the World of Spirit. May our minds awaken to a deeper understanding of this Great Truth, that we may be guided in appreciation of the great art of Mediumship. May we guard and reverence this demonstrator of our Cause. May the eager expectancy that led us into this dawning Truth be rewarded by the kindling of the flame of consciousness of the nearness of the great Summerland to us. May we eagerly and earnestly seek the great riches which this beautiful Truth holds and be capable of visioning what its acceptance can mean to us through living its beautiful philosophy. Amen.

Easter

"And if Christ be not risen, then is our preaching vain and your faith is also vain."

Easter is the story of the Cross and the Crown: of Effort and Reward: of Resurrection.

At this Season, we tender our tribute of praise for the resurrection of the Springtime, for its lessons that give birth to everlasting hope. As Mother Earth at Eastertide dons her robes of Spring, having faith in the productivity of the soil, so Jesus donned His robe of Immortality having faith in the persistence of the soul.

Easter has a universal significance, but the keynote is found in the idea of Resurrection. It proves that the personal identity of the individual continues after death. Jesus' rising from the dead impinged upon the consciousness of man the fact that life includes a resurrection for all. His demonstration of this important cycle in mortals' eternal existence is proof of the continuity of life and the basis of man's conviction that Immortality is a fact. This episode transmuted faith into knowledge. It unlocked the doors of the soul to trust, hope, knowledge and wisdom, through the proof that death could not conquer, nor the tomb imprison.

INVOCATION AND READING No. 12

Man has ever lived in Eternity. Throughout eons of time countless millions have preceded us. All mankind did not begin life at the same time, have not lived under like conditions, why should all mankind be resurrected at one time, or under like conditions? Nothing in Nature lends proof to such a theory. Natural Law demonstrates that in each day, each year, each life, the cycle of birth, death and rebirth are constantly taking place.

Why was Jesus crucified and resurrected? To expiate our errors? No,—so the great Christ Principle which He taught and so ably exemplified, might forever endure.

The Easter Story carries many significant lessons for the Spiritualist and demonstrates several phases of mediumship.

Prophecy: "Today thou shalt be with me in Paradise."
Levitation: In the lifting of the stone.
Apportism: In the disappearance of His Body.
Materialization: When He appeared before His disciples.
Independent Voice: When He spoke to His disciples—all governed by Natural Law. If demonstrations of Psychic Phenomena today are not produced through manipulation of the same law, the same Spirit Power—why did He say: "Greater things than these shall ye do." "Go thou and do likewise."

He demonstrated qualities that prepare the inner self for spiritual mediumship, viz.: unselfish love, boundless sacrifice, endurance, courage, serenity and loyalty.

"I have overcome the world!" Death held no fear for Him. Life is universal and persistent. Earthly life is but a moment in Eternal Time. This thought must have been embedded in His inner consciousness. Does it not account for the calm and composure that quietly steals o'er one when the shades of eventide begin to fall?

When about to bid adieu to Earth, Daniel Webster exclaimed, "I still live."

John G. Whittier said: "Goodbye, Give my love to the world."
Victor Hugo said: "I shall go to work again in the morning."
Robert Browning excaimed: "Never say to me that I am dead."
The thought of immortality was music to their souls.

Eastertide occurs in the existence of all mankind causing life to break into eternal bloom.

Invocation and Reading No. 13

Thanksgiving

Invocation

O Great Infinite Spirit of the Universe, in this cloistered hour when we are privileged to commune with our seen and unseen friends, may our souls be bathed in the peace of the hour, the sympathy, understanding and friendliness of those around us. May we bring our busy trouble-ridden lives into such mental poise and inner quietude that our interest in life may be rekindled and re-strengthened. May we have such constancy and fortitude that on the morrow, when the daily wheels of life wear ruts in our souls, new avenues of helpfulness will open to our vision and expression, through which will pour our gratitude for all the blessings and lessons of life. May we be truly thankful for this beautiful Truth of Spiritualism that enables us to study the seeming mysteries of life and assists us in understanding the method and object of the manifestations of Spirit and Spirit Power. May communication between the two worlds of expression be mutually beneficial. Amen.

Reading—Thanksgiving

Let us give thanks for health, home, children, friends, comforts, kindly words and deeds, happy thoughts and guidance in our daily work.

Let us give thanks for the Pilgrim Spiritualists who so bravely forsook traditional religions, creedal theologies, public opinion—yea, even families and friends, encountering prejudice, scorn and criticism to explore, through spirit contact, that great New Country revealed through the psychic gifts of the little Fox sisters.

May we ever be mindful of the hardships, prayers and labor they lived that the barriers of hypocritical observance of old customs, hide-bound religion and dearth of opportunity for spiritual self-expression might be forever broken down.

Let us give thanks for their undaunted allegiance to Truth; their ignoring time-honored dogmas, superstitions and fears in their perseverance to prove inter-communication between incarnate and decarnate spirit entities, a fact. No disappointment, no sacrifice, no ridicule was too great to deter their efforts in blazing the trail that established Modern Spiritualism as the emancipator of all religions.

How reverently thankful we should be for that pioneer pilgrim spirit that has given mankind proof of spirit return, spirit communication, continuity of life and a permanent home beyond the Western Gate.

All mortals are spiritual pilgrims.

The pioneer Spiritualists were dauntless in exploring the Spirit World, giving their findings to mankind, proving to the intelligent unbiased thinking individual that creeds, tenets and rituals can be obliterated from mind and conscience in exchanging dogma for scientific proof. Through their untiring efforts the blessed Gospel of Spiritualism has given the world a sensible, logical understanding of Heaven and Hell, a more understandable and more acceptable idea of God, proof of immediate resurrection at transition, has taken the sting and fear from death, has answered man's eternal question regarding his future state, has proven it is the Beacon Light of Hope illuminating our pathway to the Spirit World.

For this knowledge and these blessings that bring such gladness into the human heart, we offer—Thanks.

May we ever graciously remember all who have given so liberally of their time, loyalty and ability! They have sown bountifully, may they reap abundantly!

Benediction

May the issues of our lives harmonize with Natural Law and our Gospel of Spiritualism advance throughout the entire world, until All can say: "In the Name of Truth, Amen."

Invocation and Reading No. 14
Christmas

Invocation

O Great Infinite Spirit, as man is caught up in the spirit of the happiest time of the year, grant to all, wisdom and willingness to make proper preparations to receive and value the unspeakable gift of Divine Love—the gift to all peoples. May the joyous spirit of the glad Yule Season suffuse mortals' communion with the spirit world with compelling assurance that departed loved ones still live and love as before. May the glow of spiritual understanding warm human hearts with brotherly, spiritual Love. May the ceaseless Christmas Spirit of Peace, Good Will on Earth, wholly possess the Earth, reigning in the hearts of all. May the spirit of this occasion bring man ever closer and closer to his beloved in spirit, and into his life the Eternal things of this Blessed Season. Amen.

Reading—Christmas

"That which we look on with unselfish love,
And true humility is surely ours,
Even as a lake looks at the stars above
And makes within itself a heaven of stars."—Brainard.

At Christmastide elusive things are lost sight of in the overpowering touch of Humility, the commonplace things of life transformed by the radiance of Love, and Brotherhood confirmed through noble desires, lovable attitudes and honest dealings.

The Spirit of Christmas lies in Humility and Love. It came of lowly origin when the Babe born in the manger heralded an Era of Love, awakening mankind to a realization that the great pendulum of Love, not earthly gain or power, regulates the eternal in human lives.

"For Love is Heaven and Heaven is Love."—Sir Walter Scott.

Love is the universal attribute governing the state of consciousness called Heaven. It is the universal gift in reach of all. The Bethlehem Child brought this gift into the world and invested it here for the benefit of all mankind.

In every gift He gave to His fellowman there was something of

INVOCATION AND READING No. 14

Himself that made it precious—His thought, His sympathy, His vital power.

Bethlehem's story uplifts and cheers. It prompts gift-giving. In trying to make others happy, we find happiness ourselves. The true spirit of this occasion lies in thoughtfulness, in kindness, in sacrifice, in service, for He proved—"the gift without the giver is bare." Its true significance should sink ever deeper and deeper into man's consciousness, as it has immortalized for all time in the hearts and minds of humanity, the eternal quality of Love.

Love is the mysterious cord binding all together.

Jesus said: "Love ye one another."

Paul stressed the greatness of Love.

Peter said: "Above all things have fervent love among yourselves."

John said: "God Is Love."

To love abundantly is to live abundantly, to exercise Love and Humility.

Scriptural history reveals the heralding of Jesus' birth to the humble shepherds—not to King David. The Wise Men were guided to Him in a humble way—by a star. Mary and Joseph, his parents, were humble people. He lived humbly, chose a humble occupation and surrounded Himself with people from the humble walks of life. Yet,—He left a record that has never been equalled in power to enrich and ennoble mankind.

True greatness lies in humbleness of heart, in Love for our fellowman.

Love, radiating from Spirit, prompts us, at this Season, to assist the less fortunate. Ever since the Magi bestowed gifts upon the Babe of Bethlehem, man has been aware that consciously or unconsciously he is hanging gifts on the great tree of Immortality—in the life he lives.

"There's a star to guide the humble,
Trust in Truth and do the right."

Modern Spiritualism
Verna K. Kuhlig

"I beheld a golden portal in the vision of my slumber,

And from it streamed the radiance of a never setting day;

Whilst angels, tall and beautiful, and countless, without number,

Were giving gladome greeting to all who came that way.

And the gate, forever swinging, made no grating, no harsh ringing,

Melodious as the singing of one that we adore;

And I heard the chorus swelling, grand beyond a mortal's telling,

And the burden of that chorus was

Hope's glad word 'evermore!'"

Psalms of Life—(Emma Hardinge)

On March thirty-first, the Anniversary of Modern Spiritualism is observed. In the year of 1848, tiny raps manifesting through the mediumship of the Fox Sisters at Hydesville, New York, announced to the world an intelligence personified beyond the grave. An intelligence that was accepted as based on Natural Law and not miraculous or supernatural as heretofore had been accepted. This is the fact that distinguishes Modern from Ancient Spiritualism.

There have always been spirit manifestations and we need but refer to races of the past; religious leaders and sensitives who were guided by the voices from *Beyond*. Just recently the birthday of Joan of Arc was celebrated in Domremy, Lorraine, France, where in the Chehu woods, she "heard the voices"; the command to lead the French armies against the British invaders.

On the twenty-ninth of January was celebrated the Anniversary of Emanuel Swedenborg, a remarkable Seer of pioneer days, who was the first to conceive the spirit world as a realm of law. The spiritual manifestations of Edward Irving from 1830 to 1833 and the Shakers from 1937 to 1844 paved the way for the Hydesville manifestations. Sir Arthur Conan Doyle, in *The History of Spiritualism*, in speaking of the Shakers and their spirit visitors, "When the spirits left they informed their hosts that they were going, but that presently

THE OLD FOX COTTAGE, HYDESVILLE, N. Y.
(Removed to Lily Dale assembly grounds, Lily Dale, N. Y., 1916)
Destroyed by fire September 21st, 1955

ANNIVERSARY SERVICES

they would return and that when they did so they would pervade the world and enter the palace as well as the cottage."

Just four years later, we find the strange happenings in the Fox cottage and Elder Evans and another Shaker visiting the home, where they were greeted with great enthusiasm from the unseen guests.

The scene is laid at Hydesville, Wayne County, New York; a small frame cottage where lived Mr. John Fox, his wife Margaret and two young daughters, Margaretta aged fifteen and Kate aged eleven. An elder daughter Leah was living in Rochester where she was teaching music, and a son David was also away from home. The manifestations occurring at this time are known the world over. The code established between the sisters and the unseen guests; the mystery of the pedlar, Charles B. Rosna as it was revealed through the raps and later verified by the discovery of the pedlar's pack. Not until Nov. 22, 1904, was the skeleton unearthed, at the time when school children were playing in the cottage and the walls caved in revealing the mystery of the murder.

Turning to a former issue of THE NATIONAL SPIRITUALIST, we find an interesting article written by the late Rev. Thomas Grimshaw in which he tells us how the idea of the Anniversary of Modern Spiritualism was first suggested. In a letter written by Mr. James Lawrence on May 2, 1870 at Cleveland, Ohio, he states how, on Nov. 12, 1869, he received the following communication through the spirit-dial known as Prof. Hare's dial.

"Some acknowledgment should be made of the most glorious change, the advent of which has never yet been celebrated as a matter of public rejoicing by the assembled multitudes of Spiritualists throughout the land. Shall all the minor circumstances of earth-life have their days of commemoration, and this glorious, new, and holy dispensation be neglected? It is time some such tribute should be paid to those who have thus presented to the world a means of emancipation from error, such as will meet the requirements of all— a day of universal jubilee, to be observed through all coming time."

This communication was presented at the National Convention the following year in the form of a resolution *on the advice of spirit friends and my own convictions.* So we are indebted to Mr. James Lawrence, the instrument through whom this communication was given and through whose effort a resolution was passed inaugurating

March 31 as the Commemoration of the Advent of Modern Spiritualism.

The resolution adopted by the convention was as follows:

"Whereas Spiritualism has become a power in the land and may be deemed the great growing religious idea of the country; and,

"Whereas, It is well to revert to the time of small beginnings and hold in remembrance the first pioneers in this Spiritual movement; therefore,

"Resolved, That this convention recommend to all State conventions and local societies to make the time of the appearance of the Hydesville rappings an anniversary day, the services of that day to be conducted in each locality as may be deemed most practical."

The resolution was unanimously adopted and in response the 31st of March, 1870, was almost universally observed.

The Hydesville Cottage and Pedlar's pack may be seen at Lily Dale Camp, New York.

On January twenty-fifth, we celebrate the Anniversary of the founding of the Spiritualist Children's Progressive Lyceum by Andrew Jackson Davis, 1863. The wonderful revelation that he had of the teaching and training of the children in the spirit world and his desire to give the child the same advantage and privilege in this plane of existence.

It opened a new world to the adult as well as the child; to break the bonds of ignorance and superstitions of old religious ideas. That the child was a *repository of infinite possibilities* and not born in sin and but needed training and an avenue of expression.

Spiritualism, in its entirety, has so much to offer. So many valiant men and women have made invaluable contributions to make the history of this organization. The fundamental principles, based on the Declaration of Principles as adopted by the Parent Body, The National Spiritualist Association of Churches, give us a working hypothesis. If this thought is predominant, there need be no ceremonial rites observed, such as are too often borrowed from other religious denominations, for effect and to attract attention.

Know ye the Truth and the Truth shall make you free. The Truth must be recognized from within and if we live this Truth as we know it, believe it and affirm it, the ceremony need not be ornamented merely to attract. We who believe,—how well we know when at the *evening time of life,* or at any time when the call may come, that no one can save us, that no one can stay our time, but unflinchingly, unafraid and gladly do we go to meet our loved ones and journey to our heavenly homes. Merely moving into *another room,* as has been said, and quoting from Lilian Whiting,—*Life here and life hereafter is all one Life, whose continuity of consciousness is unbroken by that mere change in form, whose process we call Death.*

For references on *History of Spiritualism,* refer to *Modern American Spiritualism* by Emma Hardinge, *History of Spiritualism* by Sir Arthur Conan Doyle, N.S.A.C. Correspondence Course.

Anniversary Services of Modern Spiritualism

America
Invocation
Poem

GRAND HALLELUJAH CHORUS

(Composed in spirit-life by John Pierpont and given by Miss Lizzie Doten)

We have come unto the mountain and the city of our God,
To the ways of truth and beauty by the souls perfected trod,
And the resurrection trumpet shall not wake us from the sod,
    As we go marching on.

    Glory, glory, Hallelujah!
    Glory, glory, Hallelujah!
    Glory, glory, Hallelujah!
        As we go marching on.

Break the bread of consolation to the souls oppressed with care,
For in our Father's mansions there is bread enough to spare,
And none need faint with hunger, while we have such blessed fare,
    As we go marching on.

    Chorus

Set the little children marching, with their banners in their hands,
And drill them into service with the brave old veteran bands,
Till the tramping of our army shall be heard in distant lands,
    As we go marching on.

    Chorus

Then shout your loud Hosannas to the lands beyond the sea,
Till the people of all nations are through the truth made free,
And join the swelling chorus in our song of Jubilee,
    As we go marching on.

    Chorus

From, *History of American Spiritualism,*
By Emma Hardinge.

Address

It is a time-honored custom among the nations of the earth to celebrate the birthday of great and good personages and to set aside as holidays those dates which mark important events, national, political and religious, so that they may be annually observed with appropriate ceremonies, thus to perpetuate their remembrances and to secure for them the respect and veneration which their merits demand.

So we are gathered here today to celebrate a most important event which happened in a humble cottage in the obscure village of Hydesville, in the State of New York, on the 31st day of March, in the year 1848—an event which was the beginning of the now world-wide religious and scientific movement known as Modern Spiritualism. It was on this day and in this home, as you well know, that intelligent communication was established between the young Fox sisters, who were mediums, and then lived in this cottage with their parents, and the de-carnate spirit of a man who some years before had been murdered there.

In every civilized country on the face of the globe this golden dawn of a new era is annually commemorated. The professed Spiritualists, it is true, are still comparatively few; but the work of demonstrating the fact of the continuity of human life has been going on silently yet potentially, and there are thousands upon thousands of people who are convinced of the genuineness of spirit phenomena and the philosophy underlying them, who still lack the courage to make the avowal. The time, however, is not very far distant when multitudes of grateful people will celebrate with praise and thanksgiving the birth of this new dispensation, which gave us facts for promises and knowledge for faith.

It is the mission of Spiritualism to revolutionize the world; to sweep away the accumulated rubbish of centuries of ignorance and superstition. It has come into the world as a light-bearer to those who sit in the midst of darkness and desolation, revealing unto them "a new heaven and a new earth wherein dwelleth righteousness." It has come in answer to the earnest, intense longing of human hearts everywhere, and has shown that there is a higher and diviner life within the reach of all; that none are so unfortunately circumstanced—not even the lowest and most degraded of all humanity—but that there is within each a spark of divinity which shall ultimately triumph over all untoward environments and bring forth, from the crude and chrysalis condition, the perfect man, the aspiring and ascending angel. It has come as a messenger of light and gladness to the bereaved and desolate, who, like Rachel of old, are mourning for their loved ones and refuse to be comforted. It has rolled away the stone from the sepulchers, and has said unto the mourning: "Behold! your beloved ones have arisen." With the light of eternal truth it has demonstrated the existence of the spiritual world of life and beauty lying all around you, awaiting the coming of this angel to give you spiritual sight and hearing, that you might perceive its divine harmonies.

As the click of the Morse telegraphic instrument, when it spelled out the words, "What hath God wrought?"—the first message sent over the wire—foreshadowed the doom of man's fixed ideas of intercommunication, so the raps at Hydesville presaged the passage of many fallacious theological doctrines which had for centuries been taught to be infallible truths. A new gospel of love, justice and mercy supplanted the old dogmas of a wrathful God and eternal punishment. Voices from the spirit side echoed songs of gratitude and happiness that there was still another chance for earth's unfortunate children to retrieve their mistakes and commence a new and higher life.

These spirit messages spread with lightning rapidity over the whole civilized world. They are the leaven of truth which shall eventually permeate all systems of religious thought, all forms of government and all forms of scientific research, shaping and molding them so as to give the highest expression to all that is noble and divine in man. Since the advent of Modern Spiritualism, four millions of human beings, who were bought and sold as the beasts of the field, have been liberated from the shackles of slavery by liberty-loving spirits, who, through the medium, Nettie Maynard, counseled that grand, wise and tender-hearted man, Abraham Lincoln, to issue the Emancipation Proclamation. Furthermore, Alexander the Second, of Russia, also freed twenty millions of serfs by request of his spirit father, Nicholas the First. That great genius, Thomas A. Edison, to whom the world is indebted for so many valuable inventions, said on one occasion: "Our brains are like records that take impressions from environment. We get nothing from within. People say that I have created things; I have never created anything. I get impressions from the universe at large and work them out."

Men are not always conscious of being guided by unseen powers. Many would scowl at the very suggestion. Yet conscious or not, humanity at large represents only the outward effects of the great invisible world of cause operating upon and through it. That there always have been people who recognized spiritual guidance and direction, history clearly proves. Through all the ages of the past of which mankind has any record, be it either the written testimony of reliable witnesses, or the legendary fragments transmitted verbally from parents to children, through successive generations, history has revealed the fact of spirit communications having been received by all nations and peoples on the planet.

It has been reserved for the spiritual man and woman of the present to obtain clearer views, more perfect knowledge, loftier ideals and conceptions of life, physical and spiritual, than those of any preceding age. The invisible world is daily becoming more visible and real, and its divine harmonies are vibrating through every sympathetic heart-throb of those whose souls are attuned to its receptivity.

In the daily experience of every individual come little things, unimportant in themselves, but often freighted with much weal or woe to one or many. The spirit friends voice their messages in various and often peculiar ways. It may be a careless word spoken without thought or meaning by some friends and yet prove a message to you sufficient to change the whole current of your life. It may be a song or a strain of music from some grand organ that spoke to you, more than anthem or sermon because it voiced the guardian angel's message in a language you could understand and interpret.

In all the departments of life, in every issue involving the highest interest of mankind, the influence of Spiritualism has entered with its benign and progressive light. Beginning at the fireside of a humble home, with innocent children as its evangels, it has spread over the whole world, to the cots of peasants and the palaces of kings. It has entered halls of learning, courts of justice, the pulpits of other faiths, legislative assemblies and scientific circles. Everywhere it has left a glimmer of its brightness and a reflection of its beauty. Spiritualism is universal in its application. It is no respecter of persons. The high and the low, the rich and the poor, all come within its encircling arms.

Spiritualism teaches continuous progressive unfoldment. It does not say to the aspiring mind, "Be content; remain where you are; the past holds all the ideals you need or should imitate." It says, "Use your mind, cultivate your skill; develop your soul powers;

climb the heights and fear not; the universe and its glories are your heritage; build your home among the stars."

Today we behold the harvest which the toilers who have passed on have prepared; and as we gather in the golden sheaves let us also sow the seed for future harvests.

Today holds the fulfillment of the promise of yesterday and is the prophecy of tomorrow; and judging from its manifold victories, its blessings and triumphs, its achievement in the field of spiritual and scientific research, its greater light and knowledge of the heretofore mysterious and incomprehensible country to which our loved ones departed, when the awful silence of death fell upon them —what may we not hope and expect of tomorrow? Already do we feel the ecstasy of the coming day throbbing and beating in the bosom of the present. The present hour is pregnant with the unrevealed and hidden glory awaiting the fullness of time to gladden the hearts of all humanity and fill the whole earth with its ineffable splendor.

The gates which were just ajar in 1848, are now wide open and coming and going upon the golden stairway are the whitely shining feet of angels bearing their messages of love to men. Listening, we can hear the sweet songs of gladness—looking, we can behold their radiant faces beaming with love and tenderness upon us and recognize among the happy throng the darlings of our hearts and homes, who have only gone before us, leaving the door open behind them, through which our longing eyes can follow them until they rest upon the flower-decked borders, the evergreen mountains, the silver seas, beautiful islands, glowing love-lit skies of the glorious summer-land.

Selected Singing

Benediction

Gratitude Day Service

Selected Singing and Invocation

Reading of N.S.A.C. By-Laws

Article X, Section I. The last Sunday in March in each year shall be known as "Gratitude Day" on which day all auxiliaries, and churches chartered by them shall hold a special service in honor of the mediums who have devoted their lives to the Cause, and shall take up a special collection for the "Mediums' Relief Fund."

Selected Singing

Address

One of the fairest flowers in the garden of the human heart is gratitude. Its perfume is like the violet's, rich and delicate. Gratitude is the blossoming forth of silent appreciation into thankful expression. It is the acknowledgment of benefits already received by doing beneficial things in return, without the hope of future profit. Gratitude is graceful, noble and unselfish. Its full measure can seldom be discharged in words alone; these may, indeed, be pleasing for a time, but when they continue to be unaccompanied by deeds, when deeds are needed, words lose their savor and their sweetness.

The gratitude which is the theme of our service today, is both sentimental and practical; it appeals to our hearts as well as to our bounty; it calls for words as well as deeds. It is the kind of gratitude which is due from Spiritualists to their needy but worthy mediums, through whom the noble workers in the spirit realm have given us so much consolation, instruction and practical advice.

Real gratitude is a rare virtue; it sits like a crown on the brow of him who possesses it. Gratitude is often too long deferred. Sometimes we forget to be grateful; sometimes we think our gratitude unnecessary; sometimes we think it will be misunderstood and sometimes our natures are cold and unresponsive to our benefactors. Let us not be cold and unresponsive this day. Eulogies and memorials, which follow the transition of faithful workers, come with good grace from us, only when we have cheerfully done our duty to them while they were in the earth life.

Let it never be said that other hands than those of Spiritualists had to smooth the rugged road from this world to the world celestial for our needy mediums. Let it never be said of us that we counted our gold of greater value than the golden truths and the diamond love messages which have come to us over the wireless waves of mediumship from the land of hope and beauty.

There is no class or denomination of people, of whatever name or condition, which has greater cause to be grateful for its faith and its knowledge than the Spiritualists. For us the idea of a jealous and revengeful God and the terrible doctrine of eternal torment have forever passed away. New hope and new inspiration for this life and a rational conception of life beyond the grave have become our portion. A new heaven and a new earth have been revealed to us.

We breathe the atmosphere of religious freedom; chiding no man who sincerely differs from us and granting to all men the right, in the quest of truth, to subject our tenets to the tests of logic, morality and experiment. Our motto, in all things pertaining to human welfare, is "Upward and Onward." We follow the truth wherever it leads, regardless of opposition or of standards established upon false authority, for truth and God can not exist apart.

Since this spiritual light first dawned upon our souls, we are able to endure the ills of this life with greater fortitude and its joys have a deeper meaning and a sweeter essence for us. We are emancipated from the fears and terrors which once checked our aspirations and dwarfed our spiritual growth. The truth has made us free. The sun shines clearer, the grass grows greener, the snow falls whiter and the blossoms bloom brighter, since we first became pupils in the school of Spiritualism. It has put a new song on our lips and lifted the scales from our eyes. It has renewed our whole being.

We fear not to die honorably, since we have learned the true meaning of death and know the deathlessness of human love. We would live long enough to do some good for our fellow men, but in whatever form or at whatever time death may overtake us, we know it can be no lasting evil. We can now look with more philosophic eye upon the calamities which befall mankind, knowing that in the spirit land each spirit shall possess that which it cherishes most knowing that nothing good is lost and that the pathway to reformation and progression lies eternally unobstructed before every human soul.

What sweet melodies seem to echo within us as we contemplate the happy time of our reunion with friends and loved ones gone before. It is comforting reflection that we shall know each other there, that life there is as natural as life here and that we can still be agents for good in both worlds. What a glorious privilege we have enjoyed in holding communion with intelligences beyond the border-line of this world.

When we consider that these things have come to us through the instrumentality of mediums, devoted men and women, who have given of their vital forces for our enlightenment and comfort and submitted themselves to stand upon the brink between the spiritual and the mortal, played upon by both, that they might catch the voice or see the face toward which we yearned, then we can not withhold our grateful thanks, our heartfelt appreciation. When we consider that many of the mediums, who have brought spiritual light and the knowledge of the continuity of life to the consciousness of men, have borne the slings and darts of criticism, ridicule and discrimination, then we must not forget to extend to them that moral support which their sensitive natures so often need. When we consider that too many of our best and truest mediums have for many years been willing instruments, without demanding sufficient compensation to meet the necessities of advancing age and that some of them are now unable to provide for themselves the necessary physical comforts, then we must not, we will not, withhold the generous, the helpful hand.

There is no more graceful way of showing our gratitude to the good and loving workers in the spirit world than to care for the mediums whose bodies and brains they have so often used to give spiritual manifestations for our good and the good of the whole world. Let us, therefore, do our part; let us show our gratitude by contributing as liberally as we can to this praiseworthy object.

Offering

Selected Singing

Benediction

Patriotic Service

Music—Patriotic Airs

Invocation

Almighty and Everlasting Spirit, give us a true appreciation of the benefits of human freedom; and let us never forget the lives and treasures which have been sacrificed to establish it. Inspire us with the courage ever to defend it and, if need be, to die in its defense upon the field of battle; but most of all give us strength of mind and resolution of soul to live right, and for the right and to respect the rights of all men and nations. Make us and our descendants fitting and willing instruments to prepare the way for the coming of that day.

"When the war drum throbs no longer, and the battle flags are furl'd, In the Parliament of Man, the Federation of the World."

Give unto the people of our country the wisdom and foresight to preserve every principle of government which tends to make their homes happy and to keep their souls unfettered and give unto them the wisdom to eliminate whatever becomes a hindrance to their progress or subversive of their liberty. Shield us against the evil machinations of ambitious men. Enlarge our opportunities to educate and unfold the youth. Bring us into close communion with the patriots who have gone before, that we may always be impressed by them to do that which will secure to us the greatest good and the most lasting honor. May Justice, Mercy, Wisdom and Truth, like guardian angels, ever attend us. And may the Republic, unconquered and unharmed, ever hold aloft the Torch of Liberty for the guidance of the nations, until liberty shall become the common heritage of all mankind. Amen.

Recitation of Appropriate Patriotic Selection

Note: At this point with soft music an American flag is to be raised or elevated in full view of the congregation and the following salute repeated by them while standing:

Pledge to the Flag

I pledge allegiance to the Flag of the United States of America and to the Republic for which it stands, one nation under God indivisible, with liberty and justice for all.

Salute to the Flag

Hail Star-Spangled Banner! The sign of the free
Our hearts and our hands pledge allegiance to Thee.
We salute Thee! and echo from shore unto shore
One country united! One flag evermore.

C. FANNY ALLYN.

National Anthem: The Star Spangled Banner

O say, can you see, by the dawn's early light
What so proudly we hailed at the twilight's last gleaming
Whose broad stripes and bright stars thro' the perilous night,
O'er the ramparts we watch'd were so gallantly streaming
And the rockets' red glare, the bombs bursting in air,
Gave proof through the night that our flag was still there;
Oh say does that Star-spangled banner yet wave
O'er the land of the free and the home of the brave!

On the shore, dimly seen thro' the mists of the deep,
Where the foes' haughty host in dread silence reposes,
What is that which the breeze, o'er the towering steep
As it fitfully blows, half conceals, half discloses?
Now it catches the gleam of the morning's first beam,
In full glory reflected, now shines on the stream;

O, thus be it ever when freemen shall stand
Between their loved homes and war's desolation
Blest with vict'ry and peace, may the heaven-rescued land
Praise the power that has made and preserved us a nation
Then conquer we must, when our cause it is just,
And this be our motto, "In God is our trust."

The American Flag
By L. C. Hodgson

It is no fabric of silk or bunting—no mere beautiful cloth woven by human hands. It is a living thing, pulsing with the throbbing ardors of humanity, glowing with the fervor of immortal hopes, leaping out in ecstasies of love and dream. It is a song—the song of upward-looking men. It is an altar fragrant with sacrifice. It is a garden wherefrom a nation grew, watered by the pure blood of heroes. It is a Heaven wherein the sanctified are gathered. It is the Home where freemen dwell. It is the battlefield whereon Honor strikes its blow for the cause of God. It is a flame springing up to consume injustice and wither the hosts of wrong. It is a voice that speaks with the eloquence of graves where lie the bodies of those who died to make a mean Purity and Righteousness. He who looks upon that Flag with ransomed eyes beholds within its folds the valor and the faith of Lexington and Gettysburg—the blazing eyes of the embattled farmers at Concord Bridge—the fierce splendors of the ocean that was the cradle of Paul Jones—the clarion death cry above the ruined Alamo—the prayer of Washington at Valley Forge—the agony of Lincoln as he paced the midnight hours—and, crowning all, the wind-swept faces of boys whose bodies lie today along the thunder-smitten hills of France. The Flag of the United States is the Glory of God shining in the faces of those who dream of a world made clean enough to be the dwelling place of God. It turns our sorrows into exultation and our sacrifices into melodies of service. For such a Flag true men will always gladly die—for such a Flag good men will always nobly live.

Song: America, the Beautiful

O beautiful for spacious skies, for amber waves of grain,
For purple mountain majesties, above the fruited plain!
America! America! God shed His grace on thee,
And crown thy good with brotherhood, from sea to shining sea!

O beautiful for heroes proved, in liberating strife,
Who more than self their country loved, and mercy more than life!
America! America! May God thy gold refine,
Till all success be nobleness, and ev'ry gain divine!

Spiritualist Loyalty Pledge

We, as Spiritualists, believe that we are bound to feel and manifest toward our Country the purest, highest, most faithful patriotism the world has known.

We believe that this nation was ordained and founded by a

Divine Plan, for express purposes, having for their object the enlightenment and upliftment of Humanity.

We believe that one of these purposes and perhaps the greatest, was the providing of a people, free in thought, fitted to receive and understand the great truths which Spiritualism teaches and proves.

We believe that the Destiny of this Nation is by no means as yet fulfilled and it is our duty as Spiritualists to support, in all ways, our Country and labor to uphold its ideals to the Divine level upon which they were launched.

We believe that it is a duty to live pure, upright, progressive lives, such as are worthy of an inspired Nation, an inspired Anthem, and an inspired Flag, so that, without shame and without reproach:

"The Star Spangled Banner in Triumph shall wave,
O'er the Land of the Free and the Home of the Brave."

—H. E. Wheeler.

America

1. My country, 'tis of thee,
   Sweet land of liberty,
     Of thee I sing;
   Land where my fathers died,
   Land of the Pilgrims' pride,
   From every mountain side,
     Let freedom ring.

2. My native country, thee,
   Land of the noble free,
     Thy name I love;
   I love thy rocks and rills,
   Thy woods and templed hills,
   My heart with rapture thrills,
     Like that above.

3. Let music swell the breeze,
   And ring from all the trees
     Sweet freedom's song;
   Let mortal tongues awake,
   Let all that breathe partake,
   Let rocks their silence break,
     The sound prolong.

4. Our father's God, to Thee,
   Author of liberty,
     To Thee we sing;
   Long may our land be bright,
   With freedom's holy light,
   Protect us by Thy might,
     Great God our King.

Benediction

O Angels of the higher spheres, help us to walk in the light as you are in the light; as yours is a life of harmony, so incline us to be harmonious; as your life is governed by perfect law, so instruct us to perfect our own laws; as yours is a life of love, so inspire us to cultivate love; to the end that we may be good citizens of our country and bring blessings to our fellow-men. Amen.

Service of Admission to Fellowship

NOTE: After inviting the candidates to come before or upon the platform, the minister, or in his absence the proper officer of the church or society, may thus address them:

Address by Minister or Church Officer

Friends, you are about to be received into the membership of this church upon the assurance of your sympathy with its purposes. You are accepting this fellowship in order to assume certain obligations and to express in a public manner your sincerity in the step you are taking. If you are willing to assume these obligations, you will be expected to live up to them cheerfully and honorably. This church imposes no heavy task on anyone. The essentials of a religious life and character, the principles of charity and the spirit of harmonious conduct are particularly emphasized by us. But, before you can be admitted into full fellowship, I must ask you a few questions to which your assent is required.

Questions

1. Have you tested to the satisfaction of your own mind the sublime truth of spirit communication and accepted it as a means for the upliftment of mankind?

2. Do you promise, in so far as it lies in your power, to conform to your highest conception of right, morality and honor?

3. Will you aid and assist your worthy poor and suffering fellow-men by supplying their physical needs, so far as you can without injury to yourself or family and by giving them such spiritual consolation as may be yours to impart whenever proper opportunity offers?

4. Will you cheerfully contribute your just and rightful share toward the support of this church (or society) and do all that you can reasonably, to promote harmony among its friends and members and to make its influence a source of good in this community?

5. Do you affirm your acceptance of and belief in, the Declaration of Principles of the National Spiritualist Association of Churches and do you promise to obey all the rules and regulations enjoined by the Constitution and By-Laws of said association, of our State Association and of this church (or society)?

SERVICE OF ADMISSION TO FELLOWSHIP

NOTE: Having received due assent to these questions, the minister or church officer will address the candidate as follows:

Address by Minister or Church Officer

I now extend to you the right hand of fellowship and cordially welcome you into the membership of this church. Here, I trust, you will always find the spirit of true brotherhood and true sisterhood; that you will always give, as well as receive, fraternal love and sympathy; that you will ever find here the instruction necessary for your spiritual growth. Be faithful to duty, true to your trusts and loyal to truth. Be kind even to those who may oppose you or be unkind to you, for kindness is divinity applied to the lives of men. Be just in all your dealings with your fellow-men and sincere in all your words. Seek ever the paths of righteousness and the riches of the spiritual kingdom will always be open unto you.

PRAYER BY MINISTER OR CHURCH OFFICER, TO BE FOLLOWED BY SELECTED HYMN.

Service of Naming Children No. 1

Invocation

Angels of light and love, draw nigh at this time and shed upon this child the protecting power of your magnetic auras. Let no unholy thing, no unholy influences, at this hour come between this innocent young life and the influx of spiritual grace and strength. In your wisdom, select for this child a bright guardian angel, to be through life an inspiration for good and a warning against evil and errors. Should great sorrow, strong temptation, or keen suffering come upon him (or her) in later life, strengthen and sustain him (or her) by your powerful presence. Guide him (or her) into the paths of rectitude and honor and help him (or her) to win the victory at all times over every destructive force. Amen.

Address

Dear Friends, it was said by one of old that children are a heritage and gift from God. The birth of a child should be an occasion for serious reflection. The little ones have come into the midst of life's duties and dangers at our invitation, not their own.

They should, therefore, be received into arms of loving welcome. It is a most serious responsibility to bring them here and we should not dare to do so unless we are earnestly ready to do all we can to make their lives a blessing, both to themselves and to others.

With these most serious thoughts in mind and in accordance with the spirit and the truths of Modern Spiritualism, we are about to consecrate this child to the love and service of humanity. In their tiny hands the children hold the future, which will be as they shall make it.

We consecrate this little one to purity and truth, believing that thus only can he (or she) attain to the highest happiness and well-being for himself (or herself) and be of noblest service to others.

These flowers which we bestow upon him (or her) are appropriate tokens and emblems of the unfolding graces of a noble life and the fragrance of good deeds, symbols of a pure heart and a clean life.

SERVICE OF NAMING CHILDREN No. 1

Questions to Parents or Guardians

Do you as parents (or guardian) of this child, solemnly promise and engage, that to the best of your ability you will protect, educate, instruct and train him (or her) so that he (or she) may become a worthy and useful member of society; that you will teach him (or her) the principles of the religion of Spiritualism and that you will aways to the best of your ability, set him (or her) a good example in all the affairs of life?

Parents' (or guardian's) answer: We do (or I do).

Naming the Child

The minister places flowers in the child's hand and repeating the child's name says:

In the knowledge, fellowship and grandeur of the Gospel of Spiritualism, we consecrate you to the Giver of all good gifts, to the service of the angel world, to humanity and to truth, forever.

Benediction

Service of Naming Children No. 2

Invocation

Infinite Spirit of Love and Truth as we are assembled here to consecrate this little one to a life expressing brotherly love and spiritual unfoldment we ask that blessings be bestowed upon *him* or *her;* that .... or .... may unfold a beautiful character and always have protection from the Spirit World. May these parents and guardians receive understanding and wisdom, that they shall properly instruct this child in the way it should go recognizing that the child always learns what is right or wrong from those with whom he is most closely associated. Amen.

Service

Beloved friends, we have come together at this time to celebrate the most beautiful event in the lives of young parents. This little child brought into the world through Love is the fulfilment of vows made at the time of marriage. You the parents, are greatly blessed that this babe has been given into your care to raise and instruct, that .... or .... may be a useful and helpful member of society. As you stand here you are acknowledging your desire before the world and your God to do everything in your power to help this little one—as you express love and consideration for his (or her) spiritual growth, you are creating for yourselves and this child, happiness and harmony in thought and living.

Do you now accept this responsibility and promise to train this child in the paths of love, truth and the spiritual instruction necessary to attain his way of life.

Naming the Child

As I place upon the brow these beautiful petals of flowers as the expression of purity, I name thee ...... and consecrate thee to the care of the angel friends now and always. Amen.

And then, repeating the name, he shall place flowers in the child's hand, or gently let petals fall over the child.

The Minister shall then say:

In the knowledge, fellowship, and beauty of the religion and philosophy of Spiritualism, we consecrate you (repeating the child's name), to the Giver of all good gifts, to the service of the angel world and to humanity.

Hymn

SERVICE OF NAMING CHILDREN No. 2

Benediction

Infinite Intelligence and angels of light and love, shed upon this child Thy protecting power. In your wisdom, select for this child a bright guardian angel, to be through life an inspiration for good. Should great sorrow, strong temptation, or keen suffering come upon him (or her) in later life, strengthen and sustain him (or her). Guide him (or her) ever to win the victory for good.

Founders Day Service

Hymn
Invocation
Service

To-day we honor the name of Andrew Jackson Davis and the Organization of the Spiritualist Progressive Lyceum on January 25th, 1863. By recognition of this particular date as "Founders Day" the Spiritualists proclaim that the foundation of Spiritualism rests upon the philosophy of Andrew Jackson Davis and in their reverence for this day they would dwell upon the inspiration of Davis and the great work which he did in preparing the World for the reception of the wonderful phenomena which burst upon it through the manifestations at Hydesville, N. Y.

The Founders of Spiritualism are those devoted men and women who braved the scorn and ridicule of their fellow-men and who pressed on unafraid. Their minds and souls had been prepared for the reception of the phenomena, years before the advent. We are reminded of the advent of Christianity and of other world renowned systems of Religion. The minds and souls of the people had been prepared, long before, by the Prophets and Seers who preceded the advent and whose words fell upon responsive ears.

To-day we honor the name of Andrew Jackson Davis, but we also honor the name of Emanuel Swedenborg, whose experiences with spirit people became the wonder of his day. We can trace the operation of Spirit in the life of this great Seer, a man of undoubted genius in many secular fields, he exhibited that divine discontent which characterizes all of the chosen of God. Though material position was his through his great contribution to material science yet he knew his greatest happiness when he finally made the world accept his revelation of the Power of Spirit. He left a mark which will never be erased. We honor Edward Irving, the powerful and eloquent founder of Shakerism in England. Here was a man trained in strict Calvinist principles and in a day when the very thought of extraneous spirit influence was anathema to the clergy, yet he could not contain the Spirit, it broke through and he converted his people to the sweetness of mediumship and the voices of angels were heard in the land. We honor F. W. Evans one of the most prominent and well informed Shakers in the United States. There were some sixty well established groups of Shakers in the U. S. before the advent of Spiritualism and there are extant, many interesting accounts of their experiences with spirit people, especially their experiences with American Indian Spirits. Nor must we forget the Quakers, that earnest and progressive Society, founded in England by George Fox and whose great work has spread throughout the world and which continues to grow in strength and influence. Nor do we forget Joseph Smith the Founder and Prophet of the Mormon Church. Starting with a vision vouchsafed Joseph Smith at Palmyra, N. Y., just a few years before and a few miles distant from the home of the Fox family. In this manner was the ground prepared and the minds of the people made ready for the great advent of the knowledge of continuous life. The world shattering pronouncement that would spell the ignominious end of materialism. We are souls with bodies, we are spirit now, as we shall be through every changing circumstance.

Spiritualism is founded upon tolerance in the understanding that the power of God is present in every generation and that the voices of angels fall responsively upon the receptive ears of the awakened prophets. The Spiritualist knows that there are greater revelations yet to be enjoyed by God's children and in the alertness of this expectancy, the Seer of to-day is the harbinger of light tomorrow. John The Baptist was not a Christian when he was a "Voice crying in the wilderness" yet he is honored by all succeeding generations of Christians as the harbinger of the Lord. In like manner the Spiritualist honors all those devoted men and women who prepared the way for the wonderful happenings of Hydesville, N. Y., which announced to the world that there was no death to the ever-living soul.

The full genius and the wonderful mediumship of Andrew Jackson Davis is not yet appreciated by the world, it remains for the present day Spiritualist to study his life and seek to emulate the works, of this remarkable late day Prophet, that the World may continue to benefit from his revelations. Andrew Jackson Davis is cast in the mould of all the great Prophets and Seers of history. His obscure birth and the circumstance of his early life are in majestic keeping with many of the great religious benefactors before his time. It is fitting that the "Poukeepsie Seer" should be called the John The Baptist of Spiritualism. His personal experiences and his extraordinary mediumship truly prepared the way —

again, for the advent of the ever living Spirit of truth and the reality of spirit manifestation in the Modern World.

The Founders of Spiritualism were drawn from every walk of life and composed an earnest coterie of people educated in liberalism in Religion, in the principles of Democracy, in the emancipation of women, in the shining understanding that God speaks to man through the channels of man's own soul and not through the channels of narrow religious bigotry. They were drawn from every sect of Christianity and composed a group who were dedicated to liberal thought. Harrison D. Barrett, first President of the National Spiritualist Association (of Churches), was an ordained Unitarian clergyman, as was Dr. Peebles, Spiritualism's first World Missionary. Isaac and Amy Post, stout defenders of the Fox girls, were Quakers and Rev. A. H. Jervis, who opened his Rochester, N. Y., home for Spiritualist meetings, was a clergyman of the Methodist faith. Rev. Jervis became a convinced and staunch Spiritualist.

On this day we honor that great woman, Emma Hardinge Britten, founder and editor of "The Two Worlds," the first newspaper published in England in the interests of Spiritualism, whose initial interest in Spiritualism was greatly aided by her experiences with the Shakers. We honor Cora L. V. Richmond, the wondrous orator and one of the greatest minds of her day and age. It was her Mediumship which so greatly influenced the Delegates at the Constitutional Convention of the National Spiritualist Association, the words of her Spirit Teachers are to be found in the Declaration of Principles of the National Spiritualist Association of Churches. Without a good foundation, no house can stand and the Spiritualists of the World can be justly proud and grateful to the devoted men and women who founded the Movement of Modern Spiritualism, braving the abuse and misunderstanding of their contemporaries. Spiritualists honor on this day, Horace Greeley, the great newspaper editor and publicist, Governor Tallmadge of Wisconsin (Territory), Judge Edmonds of the New York State Supreme Court, whose brilliant career was sacrificed, that he might add the luster of his name to the infant movement of Spiritualism. The list is long and it is composed of the great and the humble, people from every walk and condition of life. The great bond between them was their evangelical interest to spread the truth, that truth which was to release mankind from the bondage of death and in the words of a spirit speaking to

Governor Tallmadge "To draw mankind together in harmony and to convince skeptics of the immortality of the soul."

> God's love doth speak the word divine
> Supreme and perfect everywhere;
> And as each heart is made a shrine,
> For whispered thought of silent prayer,
> These, organized by you, shall bring
> New power to this work to-day;
> Until the nations all shall sing
> The song of Truth upon their way.
>
> Anna Orvis.

(Stanza from an impromptu poem given by the Guides of Mrs. Orvis during the Constitutional Convention of the National Spiritualist Association Sept. 27th-29th, 1893, Chicago, Illinois.)

Marriage Service No. 1

NOTE 1: All persons qualified in accordance with the laws of the N.S.A.C. to perform the marriage service should inform themselves regarding state and municipal laws, where they are called upon to officiate, and comply with them, thereby assuring the legality of the marriage.

NOTE 2: The N.S.A.C. (by a Commission or by Ordination Sanction of the Board of Trustees) is the only body competent under the laws of the N.S.A.C. to ordain ministers in the Gospel of Spiritualism. State associations can only nominate or recommend persons for ordination.

Ceremony

Minister says:

Friends, you are assembled here to witness the ceremony of marriage between John Doe and Mary Roe. Matrimony is an honorable estate to all who enter it reverently and with true love. These two persons have made their choice and now stand before you as witnesses to bear testimony to their marriage. Therefore, if anyone can show cause why they should not be joined together, let him speak now, or else hereafter hold his peace. (Pause.)

Minister continues:

In the past, man and woman have been looked upon as unequal, the law dealt with woman as an inferior. In these later days, however, many disabilities, under which married women labored, have been by law removed. Man and woman, by nature, are the counterparts of each other. They are necessary to each other. By giving to woman her full freedom, man and woman are both benefited. Marriage is for the purpose of giving to us the broadest opportunities for fulfilling the high purposes of our creation. Love is the purest and noblest emotion of the human soul and nowhere can it grow so purely and so truly as in the state of matrimony, under all the hallowed associations of the fireside.

Man and woman being equal, neither is master, but they are partners in life vicissitudes, its good fortunes and its ill fortunes, its storms and its calms, its sorrows and its joys. Each should give to the other the fullest confidence, that distrust may have no place with them and love may find everyday expression in word and deed. With love blessing the union and the exercise of kindly consideration for each other's weaknesses and each giving to the other support in times of trial, character may unfold and a sound foundation be laid for future happiness. Marriage finds its highest expression in healthy bodies, the right use of intellect and the correct

MARRIAGE SERVICE No. 1

use of moral power, when these are overshadowed by the sweet influences of mutual love. I, therefore, enjoin upon this man and this woman that they do carefully consider the obligations they owe to each other, that they act with prudence and forbearance and that they stand firm in their own honor and for the honor of each other.

(The man is instructed to take his place at the woman's right hand.)

Minister says to the man and woman:
I charge you both, as you shall answer to heaven, that if either of you know any reason why you may not be lawfully joined together in matrimony, you acknowledge it now. (Pause for answer.)

Minister to man:
Do you publicly avow before heaven and these witnesses your willingness to take this woman by your side, to be your lawfully wedded wife and promise to be to her a kind, faithful and considerate husband; to comfort, honor and cherish her in times of sickness as in health, in adversity as in prosperity?

Man answers: I do.

Minister to woman:
Do you publicly avow before heaven and these witnesses your willingness to take this man by your side, to be your lawfully wedded husband and promise, to be unto him a loving, faithful wife, to cherish and care for him in sickness or in health, in times of adversity as in times of prosperity?

Woman answers: I do.

(Minister asks for the wedding ring, gives it to the man and tells him to place it on the third finger of the woman's left hand.)

Minister continues:
With this token, the ancient and accepted symbol of conjugal love, you do both solemnly pledge your faith and devotion to each other and acknowledge your willingness to live together in the holy bonds of wedlock, taking each other from this day forward, until mortal death or just cause do you part, for better or for worse, for richer or for poorer, cherishing and caring for each other in sickness and in health?

Both answer: We do.

Minister continues:

Forasmuch as you have thus pledged yourselves before heaven and these friends, I, by virtue of the authority vested in me as a minister of the Gospel of Spiritualism and in accordance with the laws of this State, do pronounce you, John Doe and Mary Roe, husband and wife.

May the blessings of the angel world rest upon you both, may peace, plenty and happiness be your earthly portion; but above all things, may you under all circumstances have the courage to do right, the strength to resist wrong and the ever-present consciousness of requited love. Amen.

(Congratulations.)

Marriage Service No. 2

Minister must be sure to observe notes 1 and 2 at the head of Service No. 1.

Minister says:

Friends, you have been invited to witness the ceremony of marriage between John .... and Mary .... These two persons have made their choice and now stand before us to make public acknowledgment of their intention to enter the holy bonds of matrimony. Therefore, if any can show just cause why they should not be joined together let him speak now, or else hereafter hold his peace. (Pause.)

Minister continues:

Marriage is the most momentous event in the life of both man and woman. On it depends the happiness or misery of their future. Carefully then should the inducements be weighed that impel to so important a step, that the contracting parties may be sure that love and love alone, has prompted them to act. It is the union of hearts, not of hands, that constitutes a true marriage.

Marital love is necessary to the perfection of life and the love of children, springing therefrom, is the purest emotion known to humanity. In the domestic affections is found the highest happiness and those who fail to cultivate them lose half the joys of existence.

Our friends who are about to take up the responsibilities of married life must not forget that it has its duties as well as its pleasures. New responsibilities will devolve upon you and the fittest preparation you can make to meet them is to so order your lives that your minds may be free from the bickerings and irritations that so commonly await ill-assorted and ill-regulated unions. The golden rule in married life is Mutual Forbearance. We must never forget that no alliance, however well designed, can ever secure perfect contentment, for it so happens that where people love most they are apt to be most exacting one of the other.

With a people, the aggregate of individual virtues, make up the sum of national greatness, so in domestic life, the multifarious duties devolving upon each, faithfully fulfilled, make up the measure of human bliss.

We urge each not to be the first by whom the harsh word is spoken, nor the last to offer the hand of reconciliation.

It is fervently to be hoped that you will prove to each other suitable companions through life and be knit together, not only with the silken cords of affection, but with a bond that strengthens with years and brightens with age, the bond of congenial tastes and intellectual and spiritual attachment.

To the young man let me say: conserve and cherish the sacredness of home. Make it the altar at which you worship and be sure that domestic bliss is within the reach of all who intelligently strive to attain it. It is to be won alone by a manly yet considerate treatment of the one to whom you are about to dedicate your life and who will return your affection with boundless interest.

To the young woman let me say: Now that you have won a woman's greatest prize, a loving heart, guard it with zealous care, nor ever let the storm of anger arise to wither true affection with its fiery breath. In attaining the consummation of all the gentler feelings which animate a woman's breast, never forget that love, unaccompanied by true companionship, soon droops under the chilling influence of uncongeniality of mind.

To both of you let me say: So live that when the evening of life arrives, secure in the affection of children and friends, you may exclaim with the poet, "Not another joy like this in all the world."

Minister says to the man and woman:

I charge you both, as you shall answer to heaven, that if either of you know any reason why you may not lawfully be joined together in matrimony, you acknowledge it now. (Pause.)

Minister to man:

Do you John .... take this woman whom you hold by the hand, to be your wife, the companion of your life, the partner of your joys and sorrows and shall it be your chief desire to make her heart glad, from this time forth? (Man answers, I do.)

Do you pledge yourself before heaven and these witnesses, to love, honor, cherish and protect her, in sickness and in health, in prosperity and in adversity? (Man answers, I do.)

Minister to woman:

Do you Mary .... take this man whom you hold by the hand, to be your husband, and life companion, the partner of your joys and sorrows and shall it be your chief desire to make his heart glad, from this time forth? (Woman answers, I do.)

Do you pledge yourself before heaven and these witnesses to love, honor, cherish and care for him in sickness and in health, in prosperity and in adversity? (Woman answers, I do.)

(Minister asks for wedding ring, gives it to the man and tells him to place it on the third finger of the woman's left hand.)

Minister continues:
Forasmuch, then, as you have pledged your mutual vows and have given and received a ring in token of the same, I—by the authority vested in me as a Minister of the Gospel of Spiritualism and in accordance with the laws of this state, do pronounce you John .... and Mary .... Husband and Wife.

May the blessings of the Angel World rest upon you both.

May peace, plenty and happiness be your earthly portion. Amen.

Burial Service for General Purposes

NOTE: Insert Music or Singing where desired.

Selected Poem

Address

The question propounded by Job, "If a man die shall he live again?" has been asked by millions since his day. It has been an absorbing thought all down the ages and even today the question to many minds remains unanswered. Some persons still assert that the death of the body ends all; but the consensus of opinion is that there is a celestial as well as terrestrial life, that throughout the illimitable space there are places inhabited by intelligent, spiritual beings, who once lived on earth in mortal form as we now live.

Jesus said: "In my Father's house are many mansions." It certainly is logical to conclude that mansions in the skies, like mansions on earth, are intended to be occupied. It also seems reasonable to believe that the spirits of mankind, retaining their mental and soul attributes, as well as their individuality, pass on to live in homes or mansions suited to their various spiritual conditions. Such indeed is the conviction of modern investigators and we have reason to believe that many of the learned ancients held similar opinions. Furthermore, it is now a well-established fact that the so-called dead can and do, under proper conditions, communicate with those who still remain in the flesh. From these communications we have learned much of the kind of life which awaits us when the spirit leaves the body. We have learned that God is just, but not cruel, to the spirits of the departed; that we must bear the responsibility and suffer for the evil we have done and thought; and that we must work out our own salvation or happiness by conquering the evil in our natures and letting the good, the pure, the gentle and the loving qualities of our souls dominate our thoughts and actions.

We have learned that good spirits often come to our sides to prompt us to do right and to protect us against snares and evil influences. We have learned that life in the spiritual spheres is just as natural as this life, that there are schools to educate and develop the young and the old, conservatories of music, assem-

BURIAL SERVICE FOR GENERAL PURPOSES

blies of the wise and employments for all. We have learned that it is the privilege of the spirit, as it becomes purer and holier, to pass to higher abodes, better suited to its advanced condition; but above all, we have learned that the bond of mutual love between departed spirit and mortal is never severed and that loving spirits often forego their privileges and wait in lower spheres until their loved ones have left the body, that they may, hand in hand with them, climb the spiritual heights.

If you can accept this truth, it will lead you to feel that your departed friends and loved ones are not enclosed within a far-off heaven, bounded by impassable, jasper walls, nor in a place of eternal torment where they cannot reach nor be reached by a kindly hand or a sympathetic word. Then you will cease to grieve for your own as those who have no hope. Life, its aspirations, its honors, its gains and its losses, will assume a new aspect. A new light will illumine the pathway between this world and that beyond.

The glorious life of the higher sphere lies beyond us, but attainable by all of earth's children. What a sweet and profound consolation, that in the economy of the universe not one soul is doomed to endless suffering! Let us rejoice that immortality and eternal progress are the birthright of everyone of the human family. Let us be glad that we can read with understanding the philosophy which lies behind the decree of nature as manifested in the flight of the spirit from this prison-house of clay. Let us bear with patience the temporary separation, with the assurance of a happy reunion in the not far distant future, when we can all sing with joy: "Oh Grave, where is thy victory; O Death, where is thy sting?"

Invocation

O Great Oversoul of All, we turn at this hour in our human weakness, to those beyond the veil, asking strength, understanding and guidance for those who today, through the transition of this beloved spirit from its tenement of clay, are suffering the pain of mortal separation. May they find consolation and sustaining power in the glorious fact that there is no impassable gulf permanently separating them from arisen loved ones. We deeply appreciate our knowledge and proof of the fact that souls incarnate and souls decarnate may exchange intelligent thought and whisper words of assistance, consolation, love and cheer across the Great Divide. O Spirit Counselors, we know that you gladly bestow your watchful care, guidance and instruction upon every willing spirit from the very time it leaves the body and we are deeply grateful for all your affectionate ministrations to this recent arrival in the spirit world. Dispel the gloom which, through lack of understanding in the hearts of the relatives and friends, seems as a cloud without a silver lining. Help them to realize the comforting truth of the re-union of kindred souls in the Beyond. May they realize they, too, will one day be greeted by the smiling faces of loved ones gone before. May all strive to live in obedience to the voice of the soul, that understanding, peace and spiritual progression may be their halo. Amen.

Committal Service

The one thou lovest is not here. The spirit of our departed brother (or sister) dwelleth no more in this discarded body. This mortal form has served its purpose, tenderly and reverently we now commit it to the care of Mother Earth, in the sure knowledge that his (or her) life continueth. Amen.

"GOODBYE, TILL MORNING"

"Goodbye, till morning come again,"
  We part, if part we must, with pain,
But night is short, and hope is sweet,
  Faith fills our hearts, and wings our feet;
And so we sing the old refrain,
  "Goodbye, till morning come again."

"Goodbye, till morning come again,"
  The thought of death brings weight of pain.
But could we know how short the night
  That falls, and hides them from our sight,
Our hearts would sing the old refrain,
  "Goodbye, till morning come again."

Benediction

May blessed angels go with you to your homes. May they lift the shadows from your souls and dispel every sorrow from your hearts. May you all live in such a way as to gain the approbation of a good conscience. May peace abide with you and the light of truth ever illumine your souls. Amen.

BURIAL SERVICE FOR GENERAL PURPOSES

CROSSING THE BAR

Sunset and evening star,
And one clear call for me,
And may there be no moaning of the bar
When I put out to sea.

But such a tide as moving seems asleep,
Too full for sound or foam,
When that which drew from out the boundless deep,
Turns again home.

Twilight and evening bell,
And after that the dark,
And may there be no sadness of farewell,
When I embark.

For though from out our bourne of time and place
The flood may bear me far;
I hope to see my Pilot face to face,
When I have crossed the bar.

Alfred Tennyson.

YET LOVE WILL DREAM

Yet Love will dream and Faith will trust
(Since He who knows our need is just)
That somehow, somewhere, meet we must.
Alas for him who never sees
The stars shine through his cypress trees!
Who, helpless, lays his dead away,
Nor looks to see the breaking day
Across the mournful marbles play!
Who hath not learned, in hours of faith,
The truth to flesh and sense unknown,
That Life is ever Lord of Death,
And Love can never lose its own!

John Greenleaf Whittier.

ON THE DEATH OF AN AGED FRIEND

You are not dead—Life has but set you free!
Your years of life were like a lovely song,
The last sweet poignant notes of which, held long,
Passed into silence while we listened, we
Who loved you, listened still expectantly!
And we about you whom you moved among
Would feel that grief for you were surely wrong—
You have but passed, beyond where we can see.

For us who knew you, dread of age is past!
You took life, tiptoe, to the very last;
It never lost for you its lovely look;
You kept your interest in its thrilling book;
To you, Death came, no conqueror, in the end—
You merely smiled to greet another friend!

Roselle Mercier Montgomery.

COMMUNION

The wonder of death is not just the dying,
  Not the crossing, untended, an unknown sea,
Not mounting far heights toward angelic singing
  Nor scanning cold stars for strange worlds yet to be.
No, dying is taking a deep, fuller breath,
  To know life as Now—Evermore!—as God meant;
To snatch from time's altar crushed linen of death
  And to spread the white cloth of Life's sacrament.

Olla Eloise Toph.

Burial Service for a Child

NOTE: Insert Music and Singing where desired.

Bible Reading

And they brought young children to him, that he should touch them! and his disciples rebuked those that brought them.

But when Jesus saw it, he was much displeased and said unto them, Suffer the little children to come unto me and forbid them not; for of such is the kingdom of God.

Verily I say unto you, whosoever shall not receive the kingdom of God as a little child, he shall not enter therein.

And he took them up in his arms and put his hands upon them and blessed them. Mark 10:13-16.

Address

One of the distinguished preachers of this country, the Rev. Minot J. Savage, once said: "But we say, the little one's life was incomplete. He had only sat down to the feast when he was snatched away. He was a bud that had no time to bloom.

"But who gathers a bouquet and does not think the buds the finest part? The bud is as perfect as the flower. And, were it not, can it not blossom in any conservatory but ours?

"And shall heaven have no children in it? Must none but grey hairs pass through the gates? Or shall not, rather, glad, gleesome children, with flowing hair and merry eyes go with laughter through its doorways?"

What a mystery is life! How great is the mystery of our entrance upon this mortal existence; how wonderfully beautiful and fascinating is our departure into the great beyond! We wonder, indeed, why the spirit of this little child should so soon take its flight from the tender body with which it so recently came to the threshold of this life. It is hard for those who love this little one to see in this separation the workings of a beneficent law. They wish that it might have lived a long and useful life; that it might have learned all the lessons and gained all the experiences of earth life before passing away. They hoped to see it grow to its full estate and to gather sweet pleasure from watching its unfoldment from helpless childhood to the strength of maturer years. And yet,

BURIAL SERVICE FOR A CHILD

it may be better as it is, for none of us know what sufferings it might have had to endure. There was a custom among the Trausi, an ancient Thracian tribe, which we might ponder with profit at this time: When a child was born among them, the natives surrounded it and lamented over all the evils which it must suffer on coming into the world and enumerated all the calamities of mankind; but when a child died among them, they hid it away in the earth with rejoicing and pleasure, reckoning that it had now been released from all evils and was in the possession of complete happiness.

Let the love this little life inspires unseal all the fountains of love in your natures to be poured out lavishly upon those unfortunate ones who hunger and famish for a word of kindness and a look of love. Let its many demands upon your care, your patience, your willing sacrifice, now so quickly ended, make you eager to bestow such loving service upon other children and other lives. Then your darling shall not have lived in vain, nor will its sweet influence have ceased upon earth; its silent, gentle influence will be felt as a power in your life, steadily going and steadily growing with you until you shall reach the portals of that world into which it has so recently passed. Who can estimate the far-reaching power of the arisen soul? It is not limited by the material form, but only partially hindered during the fleeting night of earth. The soul is co-eternal with the Over-soul. Indeed, we may ask. "Where did this little one come from?" and receive the only possible answer: "Out of the everywhere into the here, out of the invisible into the visible, out of the realm of the unexpressed into the realm of mortal activity." The soul has released its hold upon these earthly elements and returned to the great, wide everywhere. It has gone on in its spotless innocence, untarnished by the grime of earth. Be thankful for this, rejoice that your little one is safe from the toils of the tempter, safe from the evils that might have wrung your hearts with sorrow far keener and more bitter than that which today causes you tears.

You are not left comfortless like those who hopelessly lay their dead away, for our glorious religion teaches and demonstrates that mortal death is spiritual birth, that love can never lose its own. Angels will bring your little one to nestle often close to your hearts. As its spiritual facilities develop, it will become to you a guardian and a protector. You have a little angel in spirit instead of on earth; one now clad in the shining raiment of the arisen ones. Only a little while longer and the Messenger shall come and say to you: "Behold the child of thy love, it is thine again and death can part you no more."

Invocation

Infinite Spirit of Life and Love, we ask that the hearts of those saddened by the transition of this little child be comforted. Enlarge their spiritual vision that they may be able to see why their loved one could not longer remain here. May this experience yield them a bright harvest of spiritual blessing. May they realize that this little gift of fairest promise will unfold and blossom with a beauty earth could not bestow. May they realize that this little spirit will unfold in the spirit world and become to them a guiding light. May they realize this parting is but temporary and when the hour of re-union comes, they will be richly compensated for all the hours of loneliness. Until that time, may their knowledge of things spiritual grow stronger and deeper and may the blessings of the spirit world be bounteously bestowed upon them. Amen.

Committal Service

And now, little spirit, we commit this empty shrine to be resolved to earth again; thou hast no further need for it. May God's bright messengers attend thee on thy journey to the Summerland. May love draw thee to earth to comfort these hearts when they become sad and lonely. Ashes to ashes—dust to dust—spirit to spirits—angel to angels! Amen.

Benediction

May angels of comfort and strength come very near to every stricken heart, may a baptism of Infinite Love descend upon us all and may the experience of this hour soften and ennoble our lives and enable us all to bring forth abundant fruit of fidelity, loyalty and love. Amen.

Definition of Religion from Various Sources

1. "Recognition of and allegiance in manner of life to a superhuman power or superhuman powers, to whom allegiance and service are regarded as justly due."—Century Dictionary and Cyclopedia, Vol. 6, p. 5063.

2. " 'A belief' binding the spiritual nature of man to a supernatural being on whom he is conscious that he is dependent; also the practices that grow out of the recognition of such relations, including the personal life and experiences, the doctrine, the duties and the rites founded on it."—Standard Dictionary.

3. "Any system of worship of a Being superior to man."—Amies' Universal Ency.

4. "I never doubted, for an instant, the existence of a Deity—that he made the world and governed it by his providence—that the most acceptable service to God was the doing of good to man—that our souls are immortal—and that all crimes will be punished and virtue rewarded here or hereafter. These I esteemed the essentials of every religion."—Benjamin Franklin's autobiography.

5. "I believe in one God and no more. * * * The world is my country; to do good is my religion."—Thomas Paine, in "Age of Reason."

6. "By religion, I mean such a sense of divine truth as enters into a man and becomes the spring of a new nature within him; reforming his thoughts and designs; purifying his heart; sanctifying and governing his whole deportment, his words as well as his actions."—Gilbert Burnett, Bishop of Salisbury, born at Edinburgh, 1643.

7. "Pure religion and undefiled before God and the Father is this: To visit the fatherless and widows in their affliction, and to keep himself unspotted from the world."—Bible, James 1:27.

8. "By religion, I mean the knowledge of God, of His will and of our duties toward Him."—Cardinal Newman.

9. "Religion is man's belief in a being or beings superior to himself and inaccessible to his senses, but not indifferent to his sentiments and action, with the feelings and practices which flow from such a belief."—Robert Flint in "Theism."

Definition of Clairvoyance

NOTE: Clairvoyance literally means CLEAR SEEING, but in Spiritualism it has a technical meaning and refers to psychic sight. Clairvoyance may be either SUBJECTIVE or OBJECTIVE. It is often difficult, if not altogether impossible, for even the clairvoyant to distinguish between the two.

Six definitions of clairvoyance are here given, to-wit Subjective, Objective, X-Ray, Cataleptic, Trance-Control and Telepathic Clairvoyance. The first two definitions pertain to the two distinct forms of clairvoyance; the other four deal with phases of these two forms.

1. **Subjective clairvoyance** is that psychic condition of a human being, who thereby becomes a medium, which enables spirit intelligences, through the manipulation of the nerve centers of sight, to impress or photograph upon the brain of the medium, pictures and images which are seen as visions by the medium without the aid of the physical eye. These pictures and images may be of the things spiritual or material, past or present, remote or near, hidden or uncovered, or they may have their existence simply in the conception or imagination of the spirit communicating them.

2. **Objective clairvoyance** is that psychic power or function of seeing, objectively, spiritual beings, objects and things by and through the spiritual sensorium which pervades the physical mechanism of vision, without which objective clairvoyance would be impossible. A few persons are born with this power; in some it is developed, and in others it has but a casual quickening. Its extent is governed by the rate of vibration under which it operates; thus, one clairvoyant may see objectively spiritual things which to another may be invisible, because of the degree of difference in the intensity of the power.

3. **X- Ray clairvoyance** is a form of clairvoyance which partakes of the characteristics of the X-Ray, and seems to be objective. The clairvoyant who possesses this power is able to see physical objects through intervening physical matter, can perceive the internal parts of the human body, diagnose disease and observe the operations of healing and decay.

4. **Cataleptic clairvoyance** occurs when the body is in a trance state, resembling sleep, induced by hypnotic power exercised by an incarnate or decarnate spirit, or it may be self-induced. When in this state, the spirit leave the body, and is able at its own will or

DEFINITION OF CLAIRVOYANCE

the suggestion of the hypnotist to travel to remote places and to see clearly what is transpiring in the places it visits and to observe spiritual as well as material things in its environment. While in this state it sometimes happens that the thoughts of the spirit in its travels are expressed by the lips of the physical body, and that thought waves are conveyed to it through the physical body. This may be due to the fact that there is a spirit cord which connects the body and the spirit and transmits vibrations between them. As long as this cord is not severed, the spirit may return to the body, but should it be severed, then what we call death would at once ensue. Under this form of clairvoyance there is an interblending of subjective and objective spiritual sight.

5. **Trance-control clairvoyance** is that psychic state under which the control of the physical body of the medium is assumed by a spirit of intelligence and the consciousness of the medium is, for the time being, dethroned. In this case the controlling spirit is really the clairvoyant and simply uses the medium's body as a means of communicating what the spirit sees and, therefore, the question of subjective or objective spiritual sight, in so far the medium is concerned, cannot be raised. To some persons who go to mediums for consultations and who may become witnesses in trials at law, it may not be known that under the trance control the medium is, to all intents and purposes, absent; therefore, in dealing with definitions of clairvoyance to be used for enlightenment of judges and jurors, it seemed necessary for the protection of mediums to explain what is here termed trance-control clairvoyance.

6. **Telepathic clairvoyance** is the subjective perception in picture form of thought transmitted from a distance.

Definition of Spiritual Healing, Etc.

Adopted by N. S. A. (now N.S.A.C.) Convention, Rochester, N. Y., 1909

1. It is the sense of this convention that Spiritual Healing is a gift possessed by certain Spiritualist mediums, and that this gift is exercised by and through the direction and influence of excarnate spiritual beings for the relief, cure and healing of both mental and physical diseases of humankind; and that the results of spiritual healing are produced in several ways, to-wit:

   (a) By the spiritual influences working through the body of the medium and thus infusing curative, stimulating and vitalizing fluids and energy into the diseased parts of the patient's body.

   (b) By the spiritual influences illuminating the brain of the healing medium and thereby intensifying the perception of the medium so that the cause, nature and seat of the disease in the patient become known to the medium.

   (c) Through the application of absent treatments whereby spiritual beings combine their own healing forces with the magnetism and vitalizing energy of the medium and convey them to the patient who is distant from the medium and cause them to be absorbed by the system of the patient.

2. It is further the sense of this convention that Spiritual Healing is recognized by the New Testament Scriptures and that it has been a tenet of ancient and modern religions and that it has been and is now a tenet of the religion of Spiritualism and is practiced by and among Spiritualists in conformity with their religious belief and knowledge of the power of spiritual agencies.

3. It is further the sense of this convention that great care and caution should be exercised in determining whether an applicant for a Healer's Commission really possesses any of the phases of the gift of Spiritual Healing to a sufficient degree to warrant the issuance of a commission.

4. That no person to whom a Spiritual Healer's Commission may be issued shall advertise other than as a "Spiritual Healer," unless legally entitled to do so.

5. That it is further the sense of this convention that any statute or ordinance which tends to resist or forbid the exercise of Spiritual Healing is an invasion of the religious rights, privileges and guarantees contained in the Federal Constitution.

Suggestion as a Healing Agency

Suggestion is destined to play an important role in the life of many. Faith, hope, expectancy and belief are powerful therapeutic agents. Thought is the basis of all actions. Man is dual, possessing a conscious and a sub-conscious mind; sub-conscious life presides over nutrition and is wonderfully influenced by the thoughts generated in the conscious mind. Every thought we think has its effect on every cell of the human body, either for health or disease. Anger, fear, hatred, jealousy, and despair, depress vital action. Faith, hope, happiness and kindness stimulate the life forces and promote nutrition. Depressing thoughts create disease and kill. Thoughts can turn the hair gray in a few hours; depress the heart action, making the countenance turn pale in a few moments; suspend respiration, stop the flow of gastric juice; arrest digestion; retard the action of the liver and produce jaundice; constipate the bowels or produce diarrhoea; cause incontinence of urine; reduce the normal temperature or create a fever; paralyze the brain and suspend consciousness. A thought can produce instant death. Certainly an agent like this is worth reckoning with. Through suggestion or the control of the mind, the most wonderful results can be achieved in the destiny of the human race, morally, intellectually and physically. Through the process of evolution, from the remote cycles of time, cosmic consciousness has been struggling upward and has finally produced an animal, man, who has a rapidly developing brain. He is just entering upon the exercise of this newly developed organ. A new era is just opening up for the human family, the era of mind. Every man is what he thinks. Thought messages of love sent in any direction come back in sweet echoes. They are like light reflected and re-reflected in a series of mirrors. Under proper conditions of life and healthy thoughts, man possesses within his own body all essential antitoxins to restore and maintain perfect health. Good living and wholesome thoughts increase the *vis medicatrix naturae,* and the poisonous bacilli are destroyed as soon as they enter the body. The contrary is also true; the feeling of fear, for instance, lessens the vital action, obstructs the functions of all the glands, retards the secretion of the gastric juice, diminishes the vitality of the red and white corpuscles, the standing army of the body, and so the invading host of bacilli enter and take possession and destroy life. How often the healthy self-poised physician enters the sick room where the patient is crying with despair, and sinking under the burden of fear, and by his strong personality turns back the tide of fate, changing defeat into victory, and saves the patient's life. What does this? Medicine, drugs, surgery? No, it is suggestion. There is something in the practice of medicine beyond the mere giving of drugs; even the puling infant feels it. Healthful and harmonious thoughts cool the fevered temperature and rouse the vitality, dissipate restlessness, bringing order out of chaos, and tend to cure body and mind.

It is also important to consider, in connection with the foregoing, that by inspiring the patient with good thoughts, with ideas of recovery, hope and cheerfulness, he is better prepared to receive an influx of the strengthening and curative magnetic fluids emanating from either incarnate or decarnate spirits. Furthermore, when the patient's mind is thus inspired, it is much easier for a clairvoyant to perceive the seat and cause of the disease and to receive from a spiritual source a knowledge of such additional remedy as may be beneficially applied.

Selected Quotations

Prof. Boscowan, the noted archaeologist, says in his "Records of the Monuments":

"In dreams and visions, the primitive Akkadians no doubt saw, as they declared, the shadowy forms of departed human beings, which led them to regard them as still existing in some far-distant subterranean abode."

He further adds:
"The inscriptions as early as 3800 B. C. on the tablets show belief in ancestral spirits (nisi), the friends they once knew, traversing the underworld, hailing each newcomer with the cry, 'Didst thou become as weak as we? and dost thou realize life as now do we? Welcome—welcome to our abodes.'"

Homer's Iliad, 850 B. C.:

After the Spirit of Patroclus had appeared and spoken to him in a dream, Achilles said:

" 'Tis true, 'tis certain man though dead, retains
Part of himself; the immortal mind remains:
The form subsists without the body's aid.
Aerial semblance, and an empty shade!
This night my friend, so late in battle lost,
Stood at my side, a pensive, plaintive ghost:
Even now familiar, as in life he came:
Alas: how different! yet how like the same!"

(Pope's translation: Book 23)

Zend-Avesta. Persian Scriptures, 850 B. C.

"The man who has constantly contended against evil, morally and physically, outwardly and inwardly, may fearlessly face death, well assured that radiant spirits will lead him across the luminous bridge into a paradise of eternal happiness. Souls risen from the grave will know each other and say: 'That is my father, or my brother, my wife or my sister'."

Another quotation reads:
"This life is only a prelude to eternity, where we are to expect another state of things. We have little prospect of heaven here, but at a distance; let us therefore expect our last

hour with courage. The last, I say, to our bodies, but not to our minds. The day that we fear as our last is but the birthday of eternity. What we fear as a rock proves to be a harbor."

Buddhist Scriptures:

"The Soul is myself; the body is only my dwelling place. Death is not death; the soul merely departs and the body falls."

Another quotation reads:

"The soul is not born, it does not die; unborn eternal, it is not slain though the body be slain. Thinking of the soul as unbodily amongst bodies, and firm amongst fleeting things, the wise man casts off his grief."

Pythagoras, the Grecian Philosopher, 508 B. C.

"When thou shalt have laid aside thy body, thou shalt rise freed from mortality, and become a god of the kindly skies."

Seneca, the Roman Philosopher, born 58 B. C., said:

"That which we call death, is but a pause, or a suspension, and in truth a progress to live, only our thoughts look downward upon the body, and not forward upon the things to come."

Another quotation reads:

"A great soul takes no delight in staying with the body: it considers whence it came, and knows whither it is to go. The day will come that shall separate this mixture of soul and body of divine and human; my body I shall leave where I found it, my soul I will restore to heaven, which would have been there already, but for the clog that keeps it down."

Cato (as quoted by Cicero), 243 B. C.:

"O! glorious day, when I shall remove from this confused crowd to join the divine assembly of souls: For I shall go not only to meet great men, but also my son, his spirit looking back upon me, departed to that place, whither he knew that I should come; and he has never deserted me. If I have borne his loss with courage, it is because I consoled myself with the thought that our separation would not be for long."

Socrates, born 470 B. C., in his speech at Athens, defending himself in the trial which resulted in his condemnation, said:

"Perhaps, however, it may appear absurd, that I, going

about, thus advise you in private and make myself busy, but never venture to present myself in public before your assemblies and give advice to the city. The cause of this is that which you have often and in many places heard me mention: because I am moved by a *certain divine and spiritual influence,* which also Miletus, through mockery, has set up in the indictment. This began with me from childhood, being a kind voice which, when present, always diverts me from what I am about to do; but never urges me on. This it is which opposed my meddling in public politics."

In his speech after being condemned to death, Socrates said:

"To me, then, O my judges,—and in calling you judges I call you rightly,—a strange thing has happened. For the *wanted prophetic voice of my guardian deity,* on every former occasion, even in the most trifling affairs, opposed me, if I was about to do anything wrong; but now, that has befallen me which ye yourselves behold, and which anyone would think and which is supposed to be the extremity of evil, yet neither when I departed from home in the morning did the warning of the god oppose me, nor when I come up here to the place of trial, nor in my address when I was about to say anything; yet on other occasions it has frequently restrained me in the midst of speaking."

Again, after his condemnation, Socrates said to his friends:

"Is it not strange, my friends, that after all I have said to convince you that I am going to the society of the happy, you still think this body to be Socrates? Wherefore be of good cheer about death and know of a certainty, that no evil can happen to a good man, either in life or after death. To die and be released is better for me."

Plato, born 426 B. C.:
"The soul of each of us is an immortal spirit, and goes to other immortals to give an account of its actions.

"Can the soul be destroyed? No; but if in this present life it has shunned being governed by the body, and has governed itself within itself, then it departs to that which resembles itself,—to the invisible, the divine, the wise, the immortal."

And in his "Republic," Book V, Ch. 15, says:

"Well of those then that die in the campaign, shall we not, in the first place, say of the man that closes his life with glory, that he is of the golden race? Quite so, indeed; and are we not to believe Hesiod, when he tells us, that if any of this race die, then—
'Chaste, holy, earthly spirits they become,
Expelling evil, guardians of mankind'."

Cicero, 106 B. C., said:

"When I consider the faculties with which the soul is endowed, its amazing celerity, its wonderful power of recollecting past events, its sagacity in discerning the future, together with its numberless discoveries in the arts and sciences, I feel a conscious conviction that this active, comprehensive, principle cannot possibly be of a mortal nature. I consider this world as a place nature never intended for a permanent abode, and I look on my departure from it as simply leaving an inn."

Plutarch, born about the year 50 B.C., said:

"Not by lamentations and mournful chants ought we to celebrate the funeral of a good man, but by hymns, for in ceasing to be numbered by mortals he enters upon the heritage of a diviner life."

Jesus said:

"In my Father's house are many mansions: if it were not so I would have told you. I go to prepare a place for you, that where I am there you may be also."

Ecclesiastes:

"Then shall the dust return to the earth as it was: and the spirit shall return unto God who gave it."
(Chap. XII, v. 7.)

Milton:

"Millions of spiritual beings walk the earth both when we wake and when we sleep."

SELECTED QUOTATIONS

J. W. Edmunds, of New York, legislator and jurist, in the *Spiritual Telegraph,* under date of August 1, 1853, writes thus of Spiritualism:

"There is that which comforts the mourner and binds up the broken-hearted; that which smoothes the passage to the grave and robs death of its terrors; that which enlightens the Atheist, and cannot but reform the vicious; that which cheers and encourages the virtuous amid all the trials and vicissitudes of life, and that which demonstrates to man his duty and his destiny, leaving it no longer vague and uncertain."

Andrew Jackson Davis, the great seer and inspirational writer, said:

"Do you yearn to feel a purer nature? And to be clad with a beautiful spiritual body at death? Then feed wisely upon better substances, drink of better fluids, and habitually think better thoughts. For everything which your digestive functions assimilate is, to some degree, manufactured into the fabric of your spirit's body; and every unworthy thought of your mind will long linger about and darken the vestibule of Wisdom's immortal temple."

Nettie Colburn Maynard, in her book, "Was Lincoln a Spiritualist?" relates her experiences, as a girl medium, with President Lincoln and others at the White House during the Civil War. She gives the circumstances of her entrancement and return to consciousness on the occasion when the entrancing spirit advised President Lincoln not to waver in issuing the Emancipation Proclamation, and then she writes:

"At this point the gentlemen drew around him and spoke together in low tones, Mr. Lincoln saying least of all. At last he turned to me, and laying his hand upon my head, uttered these words in a manner that I shall never forget: 'My child, you possess a very singular gift; but that it is of God I have no doubt. I thank you for coming here tonight. It is more important than perhaps anyone present can understand'."

Henry Ward Beecher once said:

"We go to the grave saying a man is dead; but Angels throng about him saying, 'A man is born.'"

Starr King expresses a great truth in the following words:

"This world is simply the threshold of our vast life: the first stepping-stone from nonentity into the boundless expanse of possibility. It is the infant school of the soul. The physical universe spreads out before us, and the spiritual trials and mysteries of our discipline are simply our primers, our grammar, our spelling dictionary, to teach us something of the language we are to use in maturity."

Hudson Tuttle, the able Spiritualist writer, said:

"The mortal life is for the purpose of the evolution of the spirit. The end has been attained. We will patiently wait, assured as we approach the gate over which is written beneath the skeleton's repulsive form, 'Death,' that when we pass through we shall see emblazoned with the light of a thousand stars 'Eternal Life.' Death is not a change of being: It is change of Sphere. The spirit, whether in the body or out of it, is the shape. The man who goes out of the door of his house is the same individual that he was within. Respect the dead! Not with crepe and solemn faces, sighs and tears, but by a well-ordered life, that reflects the purity of the loved ones, who look down on us from the vernal heights of immortality."

Thomas Paine, the English-born, American patriot, 1737-1809, wrote:

"My own opinion is, that those whose lives have been spent in doing good, and endeavoring to make their fellow-mortals happy, for this is the only way we can serve God, will be happy hereafter; and that the very wicked will meet some punishment. This is my opinion. It is consistent with my idea of God's justice, and with the reason God has given me."

"I trouble not myself about the manner of future existence. I content myself with believing, even to positive conviction, that the Power which gave me existence is able to continue it in any form and manner he pleases, either with or without this body, and it appears more probable to me that I shall continue to exist hereafter, than that I should have existence as I now have before that existence began."

Mahomet said:

"A man's true wealth hereafter is the good he does in this

world to his fellow-men. When he dies, people will say: 'What property has he left behind him?' But the angels who examine him will ask, 'What good deeds hast thou sent before thee?'"

Emma Hardinge (afterwards Mrs. Britten), the silver-tongued Spiritualist lecturer, said in 1860:
"Ask whether your Almighty Father has bestowed upon you the thousand rainbow hues of different minds, different intellects, different faculties, different energies, different propensities, only to pass away dull, vast routine of finality. What are you fit for, what you love best, where your attractions are centered—these will determine the state of your hereafter; these will be a part of the Hades in which you will dwell."

And again in the same lecture:
"Such are the different conditions of this spirit land, and over all, from the lowest to the highest, rides the triumphant Car of Progress, sounds the angel trumpet Light, more light; and above all is the cry of echoing worlds, Come up higher, come up higher."

Will J. Erwood, the noted Spiritualist lecturer and teacher, said:
"A person who has to advertize his own spirituality has very poor wares to offer. The virtue that is acquired with the senility of age is of exceedingly shoddy texture."

Minot J. Savage, the profound Unitarian preacher, said:
"Were I to die now, where I stand, on my first coming to consciousness in the other world, I should be just my simple self; we will find ourselves greeted by our friends who have gone before us. There will be no lonely and sad awakening there. Let us not forget there are two sides to dying, the earth side and the heaven side. The stars that go out when the morning comes do not stop shining, only some other eyes in some other land are made glad by them."

Lizzie Doten, the gifted Spiritualist song writer, said:
"The stroke of Death is but a kindly frost, which cracks the shell, and leaves the kernel room to germinate."

Nathaniel Hawthorne:
"We sometimes congratulate ourselves at the moment of waking from a troubled dream; it may be so after death."

"When we shall be endowed with our spiritual bodies, I think they will be so constituted that we may send thoughts and feelings any distance in no time at all and transfer them warm and fresh into the consciousness of those we love."

Moses Hull, the great Spiritualist debater, in his "Christs of the Past and Present," says:

"He who was once called a Christ, prophet or seer, is now called a medium. The word prophet does not necessarily mean a pre-visionist, or one who prognosticates the future, but it means a reformer. Prophets and Christs are anointed by a heavenly power to advocate certain government and societary changes which will better the condition of the masses, and at the same time be more in accord with justice and righteousness."

Alfred R. Wallace, F. G. S., F. R. S., LL.D., D. C. L., author scientist, and naturalist, who for his great scientific achievements the late Queen pensioned, pointedly says:

"My position, therefore, is that the phenomena of Spiritualism, in their entirety, do not require further confirmation. They are proved quite as well as any facts are proved in other sciences."

C. F. Varley, the distinguished English electrician, chief engineer to the Electric and International Telegraph Company; assistant in the construction of the Atlantic telegraphy, in connection with Sir Michael Faraday and Sir William Thomson, the first to demonstrate the principles governing the transmission of electricity through long deep-sea cables, writing in 1880, said in the *London Spiritualist*:

"That the phenomena occur, there is overwhelming evidence, and it is too late now to deny their existence. Having experimented with and compared the forces with electricity and magnetism, and after having applied mechanical and mental tests, I entertain no doubt whatever that the manifestations which I have myself examined were not due to the operation of any of the recognized physical laws of nature, and that there has been present on the occasions above-mentioned some intelligence other than that of the medium and observers."

M. Leon Favre, Consul General of France, and brother of Jules Favre, the eminent French Senator, says:

"I have long, carefully and conscientiously studied Spiritual phenomena. Not only am I convinced of their irrefutable reality, but I have also a profound assurance that they are produced by the spirits of those who have left the earth; and further, they only could produce them. I believe in the existence of an invisible world corresponding to the world around us. I believe that the denizens of that world were formerly residents on this earth, and I believe in the possibility of intercommunion between the two worlds."

Victor Hugo, the eminent French literary celebrity, in his "Toilers of the Sea," writes:

"There are times when the unknown reveals itself to the spirit of man in visions. Such visions have occasionally the power to effect a transfiguration, converting a poor camel-driver into Mahomet; a peasant girl tending her goats into Joan of Arc. * * * Those that depart still remain near us—they are in a world of light, but they as tender witnesses hover about our world of darkness. Though invisible to some they are not absent. Sweet is their presence; holy is their converse with us."

Again he said:

"The dead are invisible, but are not absent. Let us be just to death, let us not be ungrateful to death, it is not as has been said, a ruin and a snare; it is an error to think that here, in the darkness of the open grave, all is lost to us. There everything is found again. The grave is a place of restitution, there the soul recovers its plenitude, there it is set free from the body, from want, from its burdens and fatalities. Death is the greatest of liberators, the highest step for those who have lived upon its heights; he who has been no more than virtuous on earth becomes beauteous; he who has been beauteous becomes sublime."

Theodore Parker, the scholar and eloquent preacher, said:

"Now, in 1856, it seems more likely that Spiritualism will become the religion of America, than in 156, that Christianity would become the religion of the Roman Empire. It has more evidence for its wonders than any historic form of religion hitherto. It is thoroughly democratic, with no hierarchy; but inspiration is open to all. It admits all the truths of religion and morality in all the world's sects."

William Lloyd Garrison, author, anti-slavery speaker and pioneer "liberator," writing of Spiritualism, said:

"The manifestations have spread from house to house, from city to city, from one part of the country to the other, across the Atlantic into Europe, till now the enlightened world is compelled to acknowledge their reality."

Dr. Adam Clark, the distinguished Methodist Commentator, was a Spiritualist. In commenting upon Saul and Samuel (see his Commentaries, pp. 298-299), says:

"I believe Samuel did actually appear to Saul: and that he was sent to warn this infatuated king of his approaching death, that he might have an opportunity to make his peace with his Maker."

"I believe there is a supernatural or spiritual world, in which HUMAN spirits, both good and bad, live in a state of consciousness."

"I believe that any of these spirits may, according to the order of God, in the laws of their place of residence, have intercourse with this world and become visible to mortals."

Ignatius, native of Syria and a pupil of Polycarp, declares that:

"Some in the church most certainly have a divine knowledge of things to come. Some have visions; others utter prophecies, and heal the sick by laying on of hands; and others still speak in many tongues, bringing to light the secret things of men, angels, and expounding the mysteries of God."

St. Anthony, is one of his fiery sermons, exclaimed:

"We walk in the midst of demons, who give us evil thoughts: and also in the midst of good angels, who give us heavenly thoughts. When these latter are especially present, there is no disturbance, no contention, no clamor; but something so calm and gentle that it fills the soul with gladness."

Tertullian, in his "De Anima," writes:

"There is a sister among us who possesses a faculty of revelation. Commonly during religious service she falls into a trance, holding communion with the angels, beholding Jesus Himself, hearing divine mysteries explained, reading the heart of some person, and administering to such as require it. When the Scriptures are read or psalms sung, spiritual beings minister visions to her. We were speaking of the soul once, when our sister was in the spirit (entranced); and, the people departing, she then communicated to us what she had seen in her ecstasy, which was afterwards closely inquired into and tested."

Dr. Robert Chambers, F. R. S., LL.D., the famous writer, publisher, and author of "Vestiges of Creation," Cyclopedia of English literature, etc., after due investigation became a Spiritualist, writing thus:

"Already Spiritualism, conducted as it usually is, has had a prodigious effect throughout America, and partly in the Old World also, in redeeming multitudes from hardened atheism and materialism, proving to them, by the positive demonstration which their positive cast of mind requires, that there is another world, that there is a non-material form of humanity, and that many miraculous things which they had hitherto scoffed at are true."

Charles Dickens, in a letter to Foster, the author of the "Life of Charles Dickens," says:

"When in the midst of this trouble and pain I sit down to my books, some beneficent power shows it all to me, and tempts me to be interested: and I don't invent—really I do not—but SEE IT and write it down."

Dr. B. F. Austin, the Spiritualist dissector of fallacies, in "Reason" of July, 1910, writes:

"Especially should we seek to build up such alliances with wise friends and helpers—both mortals and spirits—that the higher nature may always dominate the lower and with a developed spirituality, regulated thoughts, good environment and strong allies in both worlds, we may bid adieu to all fears of oppressive action on the part of others."

Gerald Massey, celebrated Spiritualist, poet and author, says:

"Spiritualism will make religion infinitely more real, and translate it from the domain of belief to that of life. It has been to me, in common with many others, such a lifting of the mental horizon and a letting in of the heavens—such a transformation of faiths into facts—that I can only compare life without it to sailing on board ship with hatches battened down, and being kept prisoner, cribbed, cabined, and confined, living by the light of a candle—dark to the glory overhead, and blind to a thousand possibilities of being—and then suddenly on some starry night allowed to go on deck for the first time to see the stupendous mechanism of the starry heavens all aglow with the glory of God, to feel that vast vision glittering in the eyes, bewilderingly beautiful, and drink in new life with every breath of this wondrous liberty, which make you dilate almost large enough in soul to fill the immensity which you see around you."

Rev. H. R. Haweis, M.A., London, in an address in St. James Hall, said:

"I say that Spiritualism has finally taken away from us the capricious, fanciful, irrational kind of God who is supposed to judge His creatures in a way that would be a disgrace to a common magistrate, without intelligence, pity, sympathy, or knowledge; such a God as has revolted so many sensible religious people; and Spiritualism has done away with him. Spiritualism has pointed us to One who judges righteously. One who does not change, who is the same yesterday, today, and forever, loving man through all, bringing him back by slow degrees, back to the diviner life, to the realization of his diviner self; One whose policy can never alter, because He can never alter. Spiritualism has told us of this remedial world beyond."

Rev. W. H. Murray once said:

"To me the next world is tangible; it is people without persons and forms palpable to the appreciation, its multitudes are veritable, its society natural, its language audible, its companionship real, its loves distinct, its activities energetic, its life intelligent, its glory discernible."

Victorien Sardou, writer, author, and great French dramatist, wrote thus to his friend, M. Jules Bois:

"You ask me whether I believe in materialization. Of course I do, because I have myself caused spirits to materialize at the first epoch when I was a medium. And I still await the scientific man who will successfully explain, as a psychic force of which I should have been at once the author, spectator, and victim, the fact that a bunch of roses which I still preserve was thrown upon my writing table by an invisible hand."

Ocharowicz, the learned professor in the University of Warsaw, who was induced in 1894 to study psychic phenomena, afterward said:

"I found I had done a great wrong to men who had proclaimed new truths at the cost of their positions. And now, when I remember that I curtly criticized Alfred Russell Wallace and branded as a fool, that fearless investigator, Crookes, the inventor of the radiometer, because they had the courage to assert the reality of mediumistic phenomena, and to subject them to scientific test; and when I also recollect that I used to read Crookes' articles upon Spiritualism with the same stupid style, as his colleagues in the British Association bestowed upon them, regarding him as crazy, I am ashamed both of myself and others, and I cry from the very bottom of my heart, 'Father, I have sinned against the light!'"

Epes Sargent, editor "Boston Transcript," author "Scientific Basis of Spiritualism," "Proof Palpable of Immortality," "The Standard Speaker," "Planchette, the Despair of Science," and 22 Vols. on "Etymology," was an enthusiastic Spiritualist. In writing to an English Review, Mr. Sargent said:

"A pure and Simple Theism—what I believe to have been the religion of Christ Himself—freed from all eccesiastical limitations and theological subtleties, is for me the culmination of Spiritualism. 'God and Immortality' sums it all up."

Harriet Beecher Stowe, the author of "Uncle Tom's Cabin," said:

"One of the deepest and most imperative cravings of the human heart, as it follows its beloved ones beyond the veil, is for some assurance that they still love and care for us. . . . They have overcome, have arisen, are crowned, glorified; but they still remain to us, our assistants, comforters, and in every hour of darkness their voices speak to us."

Washington Irving, the distinguished American writer, said:

"What could be more consoling that the idea that the souls of those we once loved were permitted to return and watch over our welfare. . . . I see nothing in it (Spiritualism) that is incompatible with the tender and merciful nature of our religion, or revolting to the wishes and affections of the heart."

Kant, a name illustrious in the literature of the world, was a poet-prophet, as well as a profound philosopher, dreaming of the coming of Spiritual manifestations. In his "Dream of the Ghost-Seer," he says:

"It will be hereafter proved that the soul, even in this life, is in constant communication with the spiritual world, and that these are susceptible of mutual impressions, but ordinarily these impressions are unperceived."

Professor Henry Kiddle, writer, author, and Superintendent of the New York City schools, and an ardent Spiritualist, thus wrote:

"The religion of Modern Spiritualism is entirely rational and conforms to our best intuitions; it presents to the mind no dogmas for compulsory acceptance and belief, no insoluble mysteries and theological absurdities inconsistent with our intuitive conceptions of a God of infinite love, wisdom and beneficence. It is universal and cosmopolitan, containing the good and true of all religions."

Father Lacordaire, the famous preacher, whom all Paris flocked to hear, when he occupied the pulpit of Notre Dame, wrote:

"In all times there were methods, more or less rare, of communicating with spirits; only formerly, a great mystery was made of what is today a popular formula. It is thus that God proposes that man should not forget that there are two worlds —the one of the body, the other of the spirit."

Oliver Wendell Holmes, in his "Professor at the Breakfast Table," wrote:

"You can not have people of cultivation, of pure character, sensible enough in common things, large-hearted women, grave judges, shrewd business men, men of science, professing to be in communication with the spirit world, and keeping up constant intercourse with it, without its gradually reacting on the whole conception of that other life."

Dr. J. M. Peebles, one of the ablest, most traveled, and most versatile advocates of Spiritualism and World's Missionary-at-Large for the N. S. A., wrote:

"The primitive Christians were religious Spiritualists. They often saw Jesus in visions, and in His name they healed the sick. Spiritualism, the complement of Christianity, sweetens the bitterest cup, helps bear the heaviest burden, lightens the darkest days, comforts the saddest heart, and gathering up the kindly efforts we make in behalf of our fellow-men, transfigures them with its brightness, ennobles them with its moral grandeur, and throws around them the circling aureole of fadeless splendors. And further, by and through its holy ministries, we know that the grave is no prison house for the soul, but that life, progressive life is ours, eternal in the heavens."

Helen L. P. Russegue, the inspirational speaker, whose lectures are clothed in the language of exalted thought and often freighted with prophetic penetration, in her lecture on "The Light of Truth," said:

"All your acts and thoughts here, you are weaving into the tapestry of the future. The designs are beautiful, but you do not see the result until you behold the other side. You do not see the glories that may come to your lives here, for you are weaving for the future, weaving for eternity; radiating light here and there over the earth for the salvation of the world. You are saviors, you are redeemers, in so far as your lives are helpful to others. You are saving the sinner, in so far as you are leading him to loftier ideals and a purer life; you are saving the ignorant man, in so far as you are leading him into a larger and diviner knowledge of truth; you are redeeming the sick from weakness and disease, in so far as you are leading them to the fountains of health and strength. You are teaching men the laws and the divinity of their own being when you instill into them a desire for the higher and nobler requirements of body and soul. Aye, you are redeemers of the world when you are leading your fellow-kind to better living and thinking, to a higher hope, a higher appreciation, a higher morality, to a higher, holier allegiance to all that is true, glorious and divine."

Mrs. R. S. Lillie, the Spiritualist lecturer and medium, whose thought has the sweet fragrance of optimism and whose style is simple and poetic, in one of her lectures, said:

"Why can we not all try to look upon death rationally, understanding that to all souls it it gain more than loss,—and when it is inevitable, let our loved ones go out from us as we let our children go forth from our homes to school, where they will have advantages we with all our love cannot give them at home, knowing that though they are not always in our sight they will occasionally return to visit us? Then indeed the grave would be robbed of its victory, and death of its sting!"

Julia Schlesinger (now Mrs. Garrison), formerly editor of the "Carrier Dove," a Spiritualistic paper, and of "The Gleaner," a paper devoted to the interests of women, and of "The Pacific Coast Spiritualist," and publisher of a valuable production entitled, "Workers in the Vineyard," in an address on "Practical Spiritualism," said:

"Women should ever love and bless Spiritualism, for it has done more toward breaking down the barriers of sex and opening wider fields of usefulness and freedom for her, than any other 'ism' the world has ever known. The wheels of progress will never cease turning until equality shall exist, not in name only but in all the outward manifestations, social, religious, and political. If Spiritualism cannot inaugurate this reform for humanity—if it cannot set free the captives—if it cannot uplift the downtrodden and revolutionize and spiritualize all strata of society—then all the ministrations of the angel world are useless, and all the beautiful sermons delivered from spiritual platforms are only vain and empty words."

Harrison D. Barrett, who was the first President of the N. S. A. and held that position consecutively from 1893 to 1907, in his essay on "What Is Spiritualism?" said:

"It gives us the phenomena, the science, the philosophy; which, when blended into oneness, give to the world at last a religion that is probable both by induction and deduction, by scientific demonstration and spiritual revelation. It is a religious science and a scientific religion, a religious philosophy and a philosophical religion. It gives to the world knowledge of the future, and has no negatives or speculations to offer to those who investigate its sublime teachings. The theologian and Christian say, 'I believe'; the agnostic says, 'I don't know,' while the materialist affirms annihilation of man's consciousness at the change called death. Spiritualism has one answer to all these speculations, and in two words solves the difficult problem of all mankind, saying, *'I know.'* "

Cora L. V. Richmond, the classic medium, whose treasury of thought has enriched the Spiritualist literature, in her lecture on "The Spiritual Panacea of the World," says:

"Under the dominion of spiritual truth the problems of the world are solved by your learning them: no man can have them solved by a miracle, unless it is a miracle to live; but he must learn them patiently day by day, his feet must walk in the path; and if he is not in the right path he must find it out and win another. As the light shines in from supernal realms, spirits and angels point the way, and every voice beckons man toward the truth, every help is given him to heal his spiritual and material infirmities in the right way. When he has gained wisdom, that which held to error falls and fades away. Just as soon as any height is attained, the difficulties wherewith he attained it pass away into oblivion, he only beholds the wonderful vista spread out before his vision of truth and love divine."

Prof. J. S. Loveland, the philosopher of the Pacific Coast, in his essay on "Spiritualism," wrote:

"A dual body implies dual consciousness; and careful thinkers have been compelled to admit what they term the sub-consciousness, which is really the consciousness of the Spiritual or Etheric body. We find that mediumship, as a condition, is the evolution of the spiritual senses, and in action, is the use of these senses stimulated by spirit persons. We find also that the energy manifest in mediumship is the same that carries on all the processes of organic life. Mediumship brings us to the very core of life itself and leaves us no definition of Spiritualism but this: 'It is the science and philosophy of life.'"

Prof. W. F. Peck, the argumentative Spiritualistic lecturer, fearless in debate, in his lecture on "The Spirit World," said:

"Spiritualists have been teaching ever since Spiritualism began that spirit is the real substance and that these visible material things are only shadows of that substance.

"That is what we have been teaching right along, and here comes the scientist now to back us up. Let me tell you right here, that it is on the facts and discoveries of science that the doctrines and teachings of Spiritualism are based. Every new discovery in scientific research is an added support to what our mediums and teachers have been giving us through the decades of the past."

E. W. Sprague, the medium, lecturer and former N. S. A. (now N.S.A.C.) missionary, who convincingly presents the truths of Spiritualism, in his "Science of Spirit Communion," says:

"Since there are no miracles, it follows that there are no supernatural facts; therefore, all facts are natural facts. They become scientific facts the moment they are proved to be facts. Therefore, if the giving of spirit messages is a truth, it is a natural one, and when proved true it becomes a scientific truth. * * * I see spirits as do hosts of others. I have demonstrated this fact thousands of times through personal description of the spirits I see, by communications given to me by them to determine or prove their identity."

W. J. Colville, the inexhaustible storehouse of philosopsic thought, in his "Ancient Mystery and Modern Revelation," says:

"There can be but three systems of philosophy appealing to thinkers: Spiritualism, Materialism and Agnosticism. Materialism is practically dead in scientific circles; the ground is, therefore, virtually left to Spiritualists and Agnostics, who are now pretty evenly dividing intellectual territory. Of these two philosophical systems, one (Spiritualism) is decidedly affirmative, the other (Agnosticism) avowedly indefinite; and because of the incontrovertible fact that all human knowledge is only relative, there must always remain some place for a confession of ignorance on some questions, together with a most positive enunciation of knowledge concerning other matters. No intelligent man or woman can be exclusively either gnostic or agnostic, but there are many thoughtful persons whose intellectual position is one of wise caution, who do not hesitate to avow their positive convictions that the fundamental propositions of Spiritualism are fully demonstrable."

Camille Flammarion, the eminent French Astronomer, in his book, "After Death," says:

"The soul survives the physical organism and manifests after death. * * * I am all the more certain of my inductions as to the existence of the soul beyond the grave, and the soul's influence, from the fact that I spent a long time in probing them, verifying them, and passing upon them. From 1861 to 1922 there are more than sixty years. So far-reaching an investigation is in itself a guarantee which gives me the highest hopes of the scientific worth of the conclusions. It would be only logical for those who deny occurrences, to base their opposition on an investigation of the same sort."

John R. Francis, late editor of "The Progressive Thinker," ardent supporter of the N. S. A., friend of genuine mediums and exposer of frauds, in an essay on "Marriage," said:

"The ideal marriage institution, though not realized, may well be regarded as sacred, and the vast number who are shrinking from marriage at present are exercising a very potent influence, yet the time will come when simplicity in life will be the chief charm of existence, when one man and one woman, united together, will form not only the superstructure of all homes, but be a basis on which governments will prosper and perpetuate themselves."

Carrie E. S. Twing, the medium, lecturer and inspired writer of graceful spiritual novels, in the preface of her book entitled "Lisbeth," said:

"No blow is dealt at any religion; it is only the cruelty and the bigotry that are aimed at. In fact, these characters which have dominated me have, in the main, selected from the formulas of known faiths the germs that will live and bring in striking contrast Daniel Doolittle's Christianity without a Christ, and Mrs. Kellogg's life moulded and shaped by the Christ principle.

"As for the psychic features brought forth, nothing new is claimed. These phenomena are permeating the whole world. Heaven and earth have become so linked together, that even ignorance is slow to deny the possibility of communion with the dead. Our most sought-for divines acknowledge its truths, and are paving the way for a newer, larger outlook, that the world has had before. It is no longer the question of the age: 'What do you believe?' but 'What is truth? Give us a knowledge of the law.'"

Dr. George B. Warne, President of the N.S.A. (now N.S.A.C.), 1907 to January, 1925, able and scholarly advocate of the tenets of Spiritualism.

"The light of Truth is never totally extinguished. Even when it may seem for a time to have entirely died out, yet, when favoring conditions therefore are found, its effulgence returns with the diurnal regularity of the sun and stars.

"Increasing multitudes of men and women are constantly

saying of Spiritualism 'I was blind, but now I see.' Physical blindness may be due to heredity, accident, disease, ignorance, or wilfulness.

"Evidence of the personal continuity of life may be obscured by inherited prejudice, by accident or environment, by the hindrance of intolerant teaching, by ignorance of Natural Laws, or by the individual's deliberate closing of all mental avenues against easily available evidence. Absolute dependence upon others for our convictions may make spineless cowards of all who hesitate to exercise intellectual initiative for themselves.

"Travelers by daylight, with open eyes, may read anew the marvels of the universe revealed by forests, fields, pastures and flocks, by valleys and mountains, by lakes and stately flowing streams, and by the sight of human beings of different customs absorbed in varying duties of daily life.

"Journey by night over the same route will reveal to eyes sealed by slumber nothing of the ever changing richness of Nature's wonderful panorama.

"Theological teachers of older systems emphasize prohibitions made in a long ago age by Moses commanding the Israelites not to consult Mediums of his day, however styled, and to adjure all dealing with the dead.

"The historical setting at the time of that inhibition by the great lawgiver is rarely shown. The Jews, whether in captivity or en route to Canaan, found themselves often in proximity to races of differing customs and religions whose Mediums taught principles and manners contrary to those with which he was trying to indoctrinate the Hebrew race. What more human than that, foster child of Pharaoh's daughter, trained in the life and lore of Egypt, he should forbid his followers to heed anything spoken by representatives of heathen peoples who opposed his ideas, in which he hoped to invincibly ground his own race?

"If the injunction against consulting the dead was for the people of all time, why do we later see Jesus on the Mount of Transfiguration in intimate conversation with Moses and Elias, both then physically dead for a long time? Moses' appearance there makes possible that he may also have kept his promise to Joshua to be with him, and then started for his lonely tryst with death on Pisgah's peak.

"Why did Samuel return to Saul — Angels to Abraham,

Hagar, Lot and the watching shepherds on the star lit plains, with a song of annunciation?

"All such appearances happened under natural laws established by Infinite Intelligence. Life in spirit is as universal as life physical. Life of the spirit entity is endless in duration!

"Each individual makes his happiness here and hereafter as he obeys or disobeys Nature's physical and spiritual laws."

Thomas Grimshaw, Spiritualist teacher and lecturer; for many years Trustee and Vice-President of the N. S. A. (now N.S.-A.C.).

"Modern Spiritualism is pre-eminently an educational movement. We have abandoned the idea of being saved vicariously through the merits and suffering of others.

"Nature has implanted within us Infinite Possibilities, and launching us out on the great sea of life, figuratively speaking, says: "Go out into the world. Make something out of yourself!' Ours is the privilege either of meeting death as bankrupt souls, mental and spiritual paupers, or as souls, rich in mental and spiritual attainments. Which shall it be?

"Spiritualism is a religion that consists of doing good and acting honestly toward one another; a religion, not of forms and ceremonies, nor of long prayers and longer faces, but religion of kindness, justice and good works; a religion that will make life brighter and more livable, and will bring back smiles to the lips and happiness to the souls of all who understand and live up to its highest teachings."

Hon. Mark A. Barwise, LL.M., formerly member of the Maine State Senate and for many years Trustee of N. S. A. (now N.S.A.C.).

"Spiritualism is a science, a philosophy and a religion. It is not three things, but one thing with three aspects.

"So far as it deals with phenomena, it is a science.

"So far as it attempts to answer, in the light of its generalizations, built up from a study of its phenomena, the question, What is the real nature of the Universe, and what is Man's relation to it?—it is a philosophy.

"So far as it deals with the individual Soul, its nature and development in this life and in the life beyond, the relationship between the kind of life lived here and the kind lived beyond, it is a religion.

"It is a religious science and philosophy and a scientific and philosophical religion.

"As a religion it is based on the bedrock of sense impressions of phenomenal evidence. Its foundation is as firm and as sure as are the foundations of Astronomy and Geology. It teaches a grandeur and beauty of soul development in the life beyond, undreamed of by any other religion.

"It satisfies every demand of the intellectual side of our nature and it likewise fulfils every requirement of the heart."

Mary T. Longley, the inspired writer of spiritual narratives, in her book "What Is Death?" says:

"Death brings its stores of knowledge, its planes of activity to every human being, and it rests with the individual whether or not progress is made at first. Eventually, all must proceed, master the lessons, climb the grades, and press on to higher and higher states of power and knowledge; but Death itself is a function in the great scheme and body of the universe, a factor in the world's progress from which none can ecape. It behooves mankind then to learn all that is possible of its nature and purpose and to so live as to intelligently welcome its advance for the good that it can bring in restoring wasted energies and recuperating forces that make for spiritual elevation and power."

Rev. Will J. Erwood, the well known Spiritualist speaker and writer, in his book, "Spiritualism and the Catholic Church," says:

"Spiritualism lays stress upon the necessity of character building—it teaches that each person must suffer for his transgression; that there is no evasion of that law.

"It urges spiritual unfoldment—real unfoldment; it is humanitarian—Spiritualists have been uniformly moved to participate in progressive and humanitarian work. All along the line of human progression will be found, well in the vanguard, men and women who have been, and are, ardent Spiritualists."

George W. Kates, Secretary of the N. S. A., 1907 to 1922, constructive thinker and former missionary, in his lecture on "Responsibility," said:

"We need to develop a responsible humanity on earth which shall undertake its own salvation, and shall understand that good deeds are far preferable to creeds. The saving power in the teachings of good spirits is manifest today, and it was the intent long ago to apply this power to promote human progress and welfare and to release the dulled senses of men from thralldom of materialistic unbelief and irresponsibility. The proof of the resurrection is needed in the churches. The infusion of the Holy Ghost (Good Spirit) is essential for the restoration of the Christ-power amongst men; for each shall be a Christ when love and justice reign in the soul."

Elizabeth Harlow-Goetz, the highly-developed inspirational speaker, in her lecture on the "Pleasures of Liberty," said:

"The liberty to think what we please and to express our thoughts, has revealed to man that he is the consummation of all living things and has within him the secret powers of the universe. Wherever liberty of thought exists, there men have come to know themselves and each other and to understand their inter-relationships. The man who has never tasted the elixir of liberty of thought does not know the thrills of manhood; and he who has never battled with warring thoughts, knows nothing of the glory of victory. Man is never really conscious to any great degree until he has been liberated in thought; for it is not until then that the spirit puts in the last master-touch which makes the most beautiful thing on earth, a human face, lined and formed by high intelligence and illumined by a noble soul-consciousness."

Dr. George A. Fuller, Spiritualist lecturer and writer, in his work on the "Wisdom of the Ages," wrote:

"Do the good and right not because thou expectest to be rewarded for thy services with the smiles and kindly words of the recipient, but because the doing of the good and right brings its own reward in the satisfaction it causes to permeate thy whole being."

Susie C. Clark, the gentle teacher of refined spiritual truths, in one of her lectures said:

"What is it to be spiritually minded? It is to live a life above that of the mundane plane, to reach the development of powers hitherto unknown, to discover truth through our own realization of the Divine, in short, to reach illumination, to feel a lofty inspiration, to respond to every true aspiration. The height you would surmount, brother, is within yourself."

Prof. W. M. Lockwood, the able exponent of Spiritualism, in his "Review of the Rev. R. V. Hunter's Attack Upon Modern Spiritualism," said:

"A great many people look upon us as a distinct sect, as though in some way we are like the Baptists, in a little school by ourselves; or the Presbyterians, of Calvinistic creed, a little set by themselves; or like the Methodists, another set by themselves. Let me say to you, that this is a very erroneous conception, as the philosophy of Nature belongs to all mankind; the Spiritualists of today, the intellect of today, espouse the cause of Spiritualism, because it is the friend of humanity, and voice, so far as they are able, the majesty of these sublime truths, that Nature in her elemental and primordial states is *infinitely spiritual;* that all of her modes of motion are psychic; that all things grow by invisible processes; that the human intellect is the most psychic receiver in the entire laboratory of cosmic art; that invisible modes of mental motion unites the conscious soul to the conscious soul the world over."

Fred A. Wiggin, the medium, in his book on "Cubes and Spheres," says:

"And ever and forever as the ages roll, the great ocean of Life will throb and pulsate with God's Love. It will beat against the headlands and granite cliffs of ignorance until they crumble and melt away, and over these ruined bulwarks the billows of Truth will sweep on and on, bearing upon their mighty crests, the ark of safety in which every expression of human life will float onward, and the involved be borne back into the Infinite Heart of God, from which it was primarily evolved."

Mary S. Vanderbilt, the distinguished American medium, in an address at Haverhill, Mass., in 1898, said:

"Spiritualism has outridden the gale of popular opinion, the clouds overhead are broken and the dawn of a yet brighter day gladdens our souls. Though we may weep for the dead let us salute the immortals. The day will come when they will visit every fireside, hold converse with us, and sit at our table on our sacred anniversaries.

"In the influence of the bright memories of our early

defenders, and spurred on by their exalted example, may we be lifted to the mount of transfiguration, where, communing with their spirits, we may discern the sublime grandeur of the mighty truth of Spiritualism, for which they lived and labored."

Sir Oliver Lodge in message sent to the convention of World Fellowship of Faiths held in Chicago in September, 1933: "What nations have to realize is the guiding and helpful power of the spiritual world. All religions can agree on that great thesis, with whatever restrictions and minutiae it may be accompanied because of individual beliefs and sectarian prejudices. Let us unite in this enterprise of impressing the reality of the spiritual world and its active co-operation with us, and the outlook for the future becomes bright."

So let my friends who look upon my clay,
Before the purifying blaze has loosed
Its hold upon my real self,
Go on the even tenor of their way
With neither moan, nor tear, nor fear for me,
Rejoicing that the change has "made me free"
And opened up the door to progress ever more.
If forward turn their thoughts,
I pray them think of me as journeying on
In search of Truth and Love and Beauty,
With less of earthly dross and limitations,
With more of Light and Life and Power,
As I climb the heights.
And so I would that my life here and there,
Become a lasting benediction to the world.
     B. F. Austin in *When I Am Gone*.

God is spirit (not "a spirit" as incorrectly rendered) and if man be made in his image and likeness, he, in his real being must be spirit also. The seen body is man's instrument, but it is not man. Our souls breathe the spiritual atmosphere of God's imminence. Men have sought everywhere outside to find God, vainly neglecting the spiritual corridors of their profounder consciousness. As man thinks God-like thoughts and comes into deific conjunction, he also gains an increasing command of spiritual powers and prerogatives.
  Henry Wood in *Life More Abundant*.

Death is the laying down of an instrument which is no longer fitted for, or responsive to soul growth. It is emergence from an outgrown shell. To be dead is good if it be death in the right direction. It is the leaving behind of that which is no longer useful. Death to sin is life to righteousness. Such is the real resurrection, rather than any collecting of dust which once served as a temporary costume or tenement.

Henry Wood in *Life More Abundant*.

Was God nearer to the world in the days of the patriarchs and prophets than he is today? Is he not as ready to lead our nation as he was the Hebrew people? Why do men hunt for him in the darkness and distance rather than in the light and nearby? Special devotion to the sanctities of the dead past takes from the present a large part of its value and beauty. Whittier voices the spiritual ideal:

"That all of good the past hath had
Remains to make our own time glad,
Our common daily life divine,
And every land a Palestine.
"Henceforth my heart shall sigh no more
For olden time and holier shore
God's love and blessing, then and there,
Are now and here and everywhere."

Henry Wood in *Life More Abundant*.

Sir Arthur Conan Doyle: "Spiritualism is the greatest revelation the world has ever known."

I have seen spirits walk around the room and join in the talk of the company.

We are continually conscious of protection around us.

General experience shows that a facile acceptance of these claims of spirit is very rare among earnest thinkers and that there is hardly any prominent Spiritualist whose course of study and reflection has not involved a novitate of many years.

The History of Spiritualism.

James Abbott (Former Editor of THE NATIONAL SPIRITUALIST): "But let there be no sadness of farewell, when we shall cross the bar. All departures in nature are singularly glorious. The brilliant hues of the falling leaf are not the hectic of decay, but the sign of maturity. Its turning is not a mournful spectacle, but rather a joyous one, when nature arrays herself for the festival of triumph. It is her season of jubilation and magnificence."

Rev. E. W. Sprague: "Right thinking is man's true saviour. It very soon establishes his self-reliance, and self-reliance, coupled with right thinking will develop man's moral nature to the highest point and prepare him to enter into spiritual unfoldment of those higher gifts and faculties that place him in communion with spirits in the spiritual realms.

"In the study of Modern Spiritualism one is brought into the spiritual thought realm and his spiritual faculties are touched by the thoughts of spirits which stimulate them into activity. The same law operates in every realm. Knowing this we must unfold spiritually so that our spiritual faculties become active."

Man Limitless

History has shown, that in every step man has taken upward to a higher plane of mental activity and ideality, he has taken each one by the overcoming of certain environments and by the freeing himself from some early beliefs which a broadening intelligence discovered to be fallacious. In advancing he has, however, always carried with him certain dogmas of error in spite of the fact that others which had formerly fettered him were thrown aside. Having made the intellectual advance, more light gradually came; and, with the mental horizon widened by years of thoughtful observation, another and another step has been taken. At each advance some errors have been dropped, while some were still retained and carried forward. As I follow the ascent of man toward complete mental freedom, I can see most clearly that he has forged his own fetters, and that he alone is responsible for his growth.

The dawning of the new century is marked as a thought-period in history. Representative man is doing his own thinking. He has advanced to a point where his consciousness has awakened to a concept of his possibilities. Step by step he has progressed through the ages; now, at one leap or bound, he links himself to Infinity and claims the realization of his hopes and ideals as his birthright. He demands if Infinity holds secrets that they shall be disclosed to him; because he is one with infinite life.

Knowing this plane is attainable in the present age, and believing thousands and thousands are approaching it, I present the mental paths I have traversed and which led me to recognize man's heritage of power opening into his limitless possibilities.

FLOYD B. WILSON.

Suggestions for Self Culture

Things to Avoid and Things to Cultivate

Things to Avoid

IGNORANCE: This is the most fruitful source of crime and misery in the world. It is the devil which destroys; it is retroactive, and destroys every victim, in degree, who is unfortunate enough to be in its clutches. Ignorance of the functions of mind and body give rise to the abuses which undermine health and morality. Its only antidote is rational knowledge of self.

HATE: This is a mental attitude which generates chemical poisons in the body of the human. No person can be actually healthy who harbors this attitude toward any person, or persons. And the fullest development of soul is an impossibility while hate dwells within the mind. Its antidote is: Love!

GOSSIP: This is the mental habit of discussing one's neighbor with a total disregard for the actual realities of the case; it is destructive in its tendency, because of the disturbed mental atmosphere it creates. It is the habit of pointing out the petty imperfections of others and enlarging upon them. Its antidote is: Pointing out the goodly qualities of others—learning the art of being kind.

SLANDER: Is the offspring of Ignorance and Hate, and is poison to the one who indulges in it. No one but an undeveloped, ignorant individual will be guilty of this mental murder; it is death to the finer qualities of soul. Slander is gossip run to seed—it is the stuff of which assassins are made. And the possessor of the tongue that slanders harbors a viper which will sting him to death. There is no antidote save to root it out of the system—out of the mind. Slander is a cancer eating out the heart of the slanderer.

SUSPICION: Is the mental state which sees in others the vileness which exists in one's self. It is the demoniac alchemist who transmutes good into evil, and virtue into vice. Its presence in the mind of humans denotes moral and spiritual disease of marked character. It can only live in the mind of one who at heart is guilty of every crime he attributes to another. It is usually to be found in the minds of those who have burned out their capacity for excess and dissipation of various kinds. Its antidote is Faith in humans; trust in the inherent divinity in mankind.

JEALOUSY: Is suspicion gone mad; it is Insanity of the third degree. Like suspicion it is a diseased state of the mind and generates poison in the system of the one who harbors it. Jealousy is the vile Frankenstein who knows no innocence; who sees no virtue; who recognizes no justice, and believes no trust. It is the antithesis of love. Its antidote is: Faith—Confidence—Love.

WORRY: Is the moth that destroys the fabric of human endeavor; it is the builder of bridges that are never crossed. It is the trap which ensnares the human who would evolve to greater things. Worry is the smoked glass which obscures the larger day. It is mental disorder; it is the fog that conceals the harbor from view—it is the rock upon which the bark of endeavor is wrecked. Its antidote is: Mental poise, constructive thinking—Optimism.

FEAR: Is the millstone about the neck of humanity; it is the avalanche which buries statesmen, poets, artists, sculptors, master musicians, scientists, supermen and superwomen, while yet in the making. It is the dynamite which destroys the bridge of hope; it is the worm that eats out the heart of the mighty oak, and destroys the roots of the rose. It is the barnacle which impedes the ship of progress. And its only antidote is: Courage—Courage wedded to perennial Hope.

Things to Cultivate

FAITH: Not the blind, subservient faith that makes you feel yourself a worm of the dust; not that! But rather the kind which reveals to you your own divinity. Know that progress is absolutely certain—that your development will come just as fast as you have made ready for it.

REASONABLENESS: Do not expect to know it all in a day; and do not expect miracles in your favor. In the first place miracles do not happen; in the second place you would not know what to do with a miracle if it came your way. And in the third place such a thing would contravene natural law—nature does not work that way.

COURAGE: Do not whimper and whine because it seems a long time before you get your growth. Each day is a day of growth; and great development is the sum total of the steps taken in the days that have been. One of these days you will wake up and find yours has arrived. Meet the world with a smile, and unafraid; do the best you can and let the world grow if it must.

SILENCE: Do not make a noise about your growth; if you are growing you don't have to tell folks—it will show, and they can see it. Don't complain because the world does not understand you—you don't understand yourself yet! Use your energy in "getting together with yourself" and finding out who you are, and what you can do—then do it.

GENEROSITY: Do not make invidious comparisons between your knowledge—your spiritual growth and that of someone else, to the detriment of that someone else. Remember: the person who has to advertise his own spirituality has mighty poor wares to offer.

JUSTICE: Recognize the fact that you are not the only divine soul whom the Infinite has permitted to manifest in the flesh. There are others! Give them credit for wanting, just as earnestly as you, to become the "Man Spiritual"—"The Woman Spiritual." Do not be a carping critic! Point out the good things in the lives of others and Keep Sweet!

ECONOMY: Do not be a profligate with your energy; use all you need, but do not throw it away. Cultivate the law of use, and apply it in all things! Be fair with yourself as well as others. Be your own friend; then you can be of assistance to the world.

SYSTEM: Do not fail to establish order in your life—in your effort for growth. Order is the Infinite Magician who turns failure into success; transmutes darkness into light; brings health out of illness and turns obstacles into helps. Order is the first law of nature—it is the handmaiden of Faith; it will make you King—Queen, in the realm of your selfhood.

INDIVIDUALITY: Do not try to be someone else—don't be an ape! Cultivate your individuality; you can express yourself better than you can imitate someone else. There is only one You—let that one shine forth in all the resplendent selfhood which the real You possesses. It will be infinitely easier than trying to be someone else. (*W. J. Erwood.*)

MERCY: Is one of the most humane traits of Mankind. To be merciful is to be kind, revealing the kinship between Man and the Divine. Unfold this benevolent power of tenderness and service. Realize your responsibility of aid and protection of those who may need your help, sympathy and counsel in their hour of need. Give of your Wisdom to those who are ill in Mind, and of your Talent and Strength to those who are sick of Body. Teach them to look up filled with a Faith that passes human understanding. Instruct them to think only in terms of Health and Happiness, that they may share with you in the appreciation of all the beauty and grandeur of this Life. Through the practice of this "Act of Kindness" there is brought to the surface the finest qualities of womanhood and manhood, that build for a higher and more perfect Civilization.

CO-OPERATION: It is the Master Key which unlocks the Gateway of Progress, that leads to greater achievements in all fields of human endeavor. It is yours for the asking and willingness to do your part. Cultivate an interest of consideration toward others in your every act and deed. Without co-operation you cannot hope for the full realization of your dreams and ideals. It demands of you to work hand in hand with your fellowmen, toward the fulfillment of the things, which bring joy and make Life worth Living. Give freely of your time and effort to this great Cause, that you may find success in your every action. Thus, through serving your fellowmen you will find the true value of Life. Happiness and the knowledge of having Done Things will be yours, and the world will have been a better world for you having lived.

TOLERANCE: Practice it. Make it a part of your Philosophy of Life. Its principles embrace a sense of fairness and understanding toward the acts, beliefs and views of our fellowmen. Tolerance opens the doorway to greater progress and friendliness among the World's People. In its true light "Tolerance Alone" is not enough. You must cultivate a deep appreciation of the actions and opinions of others. Through this realization alone can you hope to discover the secret which makes lives more complete and enjoyable. The spreading of its fundamentals among mankind will lead to Universal Fellowship and World Peace.

Trance and Inspirational Speaking

Trance

Trance is defined by Webster as a state in which the soul seems to have passed into another state of being, or to be rapt in visions; an ecstasy.

In the Acts of the Apostles, Chapter X, verses 9 and 10, it is recorded that Peter went upon the housetop to pray and that he became very hungry, and would have eaten; but while they made ready he fell into a trance. And in Chapter XXII, verse 17, it is recorded that Paul said of himself; that when he was come again in Jerusalem, even while he prayed in the temple, he was in a trance.

Trance, as above defined and alluded to, is usually the result of religious or other exaltation; sometimes, indeed, the artist, poet or enraptured idealist really passes into a state of trance, in which the spirit seems to be apart from the body. Noted instances in the history of the word's most advanced and imaginative minds seem to support this idea.

Trance-Mediumship

This is a term introduced by the advent of Modern Spiritualism to designate certain phases of mediumship, in which there is a total unconsciousness on the part of the medium of events passing in the mundane world. This state is superinduced by an external spirit intelligence (a spirit which has once lived in mortal form), whose personality becomes dominant and uses the organism of the medium for the purposes of writing or speaking, usually the latter. In trance-mediumship, the medium passes from a state of outward consciousness into one resembling natural sleep, without any writhing cataleptic symptoms; although there are sometimes a few nervous or muscular twitchings, which are the result of the adjustment of the system of the medium to the forces of the entracing spirit. In this sleep, or trance, there are always spiritual experiences apart from the body, but they are very seldom retained.

It is a beautiful and pleasing state for the medium when the consciousness has been transferred, during the period of entrancement, to another sphere of environment, where there is often a meeting with friends who have passed from the mortal existence; and it is particularly delightful to the medium when the recollection of those surpassing experiences is not lost after the entrancement has ceased. The medium has no remembrance of the message or address given by the spirit through his or her organism, although the entrancement may have lasted for hours and vast audiences been instructed, comforted and encouraged by the speech of the controlling mind.

Compared to the whole number of the various kinds of mediums, there are very few trance-mediums. They are not selected according to any human standards of morality or belief, but with reference to the work to be done and according to the law of spiritual adaptation; and sometimes, as in cases of little children and uneducated adults, they are manifestly chosen "to confound the wise." Nevertheless, in the language of Hudson Tuttle, the highest expression of mediumship is dependent on morality, intelligence and spiritual purity.

Trance-mediumship better serves the purpose of the entrancing spirit and is a greater protection to the medium, without in any way retarding or hindering the normal unfoldment of the faculties of the medium. There are a number of reasons why this phase of mediumship is superior for lectures and speeches, but only three will be cited here:

First: Because, by removing the consciousness of the medium from the scene of human activity there is protection from the audience, which might be, and which certainly were, in the early years of these manifestations, harshly critical and strongly antagonistic.

Second: Because the manifesting spirit is in this way better able to express the ideas intended to be conveyed, which in many instances, are novel, if not entirely new, and if the entrancement were not total, the mind of the medium might be aroused to wonder or speculation and thus interfere with the fluency and accuracy of the speech.

Third: Because there is little or no nervous strain on the medium's organism, while the speech is proceeding, as compared with the strain on the ordinary speaker or as compared with that which the medium would undergo if partially conscious and continually questioning the verity of the statements made.

Trance-Mediumship Not Harmful

There is no uniformity of temperament or personality among trance-mediums. They come from among all conditions and grades of social and intellectual life. Many people have erroneously supposed that trance-mediumship causes a loss of individuality or that it is followed by detrimental results to the mentality; but, as a matter of fact, the best trance, as well as inspirational, speakers and mediums, are also the best unfolded otherwise. For these reasons:

First: The intelligences acting upon them are almost invariably of a superior character and, therefore, must mold the organism, by constant use, for the expression of higher forms of thought.

Second: The relation of the medium to the manifesting intelligence is that of pupil and teacher, sometimes that of a child to a wise and loving parent, and sometimes both these relations combined with a subtle and ennobling spirituality.

Third: There is always a mutual spiritual relation, even though the medium is not humanly conscious of it; and no one can be a medium for the perfect expression of spirit messages or discourses, who does not consent to the procedure and cooperate with the manifesting spirit.

Fourth: As the master-musician improves the instrument he plays upon, so, also a spirit controlling a human organism for the purpose of expressing wholesome thought, imparts a greater power, both to the brain and the spirit of the medium.

In many cases, especially where the medium has been chosen in childhood or in early youth, before there were fixed habits of erroneous speech, the entire education of the medium has been undertaken by the spirit intelligences desiring to make the medium their mouthpiece; but in cases where the habits of speech and thought have become fixed, they are difficult to overcome, and sometimes there remain permanent faults which are mistakenly attributed to the lack of culture on the part of the spirit. There are, however, cases where adults, during entrancement, have been made to express scientific and exalted thought with perfect rhetoric; although the medium was unlearned and mentally untrained, and some have spoken perfectly both ancient and modern languages, with which they were entirely unfamiliar.

Inspirational Speaking

Inspirational speaking is a form of mediumship in which the medium is not rendered wholly unconscious. It varies from an abstracted consciousness to a partial or intermittent entrancement. It this phase the spirit does not thoroughly control the nerve center through which the organs of speech are manipulated, and, therefore, only impinges upon the magnetic aura of the medium and wafts its thoughts upon the brain, which acts as a sort of receiving station.

Sometimes inspirational speakers are influenced in the same speech by several spirit intelligences and thus the speech itself will be a combination of the thought of the speaker and the influencing spirits.

CORA L. V. RICHMOND.

Definition of Prophecy

It may be well to consider the meaning of the word prophecy. It is derived from the Greek word *prophemi*, pro meaning before, and phemi, to say or tell. There is another word *propheteuo*, of similar import, and derivation, and means, to prophecy, divine, foretell, predict, presage; to explain or apply prophecies. In Greek classical literature, the word *prophet* means a declarer, foreteller, diviner; a harbinger, a forerunner, a priest, teacher, instructor, interpreter; a poet, a bard. All of these definitions carry with them something of the idea of a character, whose mission is in some way connected with the aspirations and longings of mankind.

The Standard Dictionary of 1902 defines prophecy as follows:

1. To predict or foretell, especially under divine inspiration and guidance; to pre-figure; as, to prophesy evil. 2. To speak or utter for God. 3. To speak by divine influence, or as a medium of communication between God and man. Specifically: To speak to men for God; declare or interpret the divine will. 4. To predict future events by supernatural influence, real or professed: To foretell the future; utter predictions, as, to prophesy a disaster. 5. (Archaic) To interpret scripture; explain religious subjects, preach; exhort.

Under the head of Synonyms, the Standard Dictionary gives: "Augur, divine, foretell, predict, prognosticate. Prophesy differs from predict by assuming a claim to supernatural or divine inspiration. To prognosticate is to predict from observed signs, indications, or conditions. To prophesy in the scriptural sense is to utter religious truths under divine inspiration, not simply always to foretell future events, but to warn, exhort, comfort, etc., by special message or impulse from God."

This scriptural definition seems well adapted to the Spiritualist sense of the word, when we interpret God to mean the Infinite Spirit of Good. The verb prophesy is also used in the New Testament in the sense of revealing something which had happened and was unknown to the person revealing it except through some so-called supernatural source.

Prophecy

Spiritualism, as distinguished from spiritism, is a religion. The philosophy of Spiritualism is based upon psychical phenomena. Among the doctrines of Spiritualism is the belief that when the spirit departs from the material body at death, it enters the spirit world and is morally and intellectually no better nor worse than it was immediately prior to its transition, and that the opportunities for its progression are never denied, that the door to reformation is never closed, that spirits in the spirit world are able, under certain conditions, to communicate with spirits still incarnate and that many of them do so.

It is the custom and practice of Spiritualists, in conformity with their religious belief, to consult and hold communion with spirits gone before, for several reasons:

First, to learn from them moral lessons. And these are sometimes impressed as forcibly by those spirits who still inhabit the lower spheres as by those who have advanced to higher ones; even as we are, in this life, sometimes more quickly moved to moral effort by the conditions and sufferings of the sinful than we are by the precept and example of those who live pure and upright lives.

Second, to receive instructions from spirits in regard to the laws, structure, and character of the spirit world; just as we would try to learn of these things in regard to any country on this earth to which we expected to travel.

Third, to hold communion with our beloved ones over there for the mere pleasure that such communion imparts, in exchanging assurance of continued love, just to do in this world, by visiting and writing to the objects of our love and affection.

Fourth, to seek the advice of spirits in matters affecting our mundane welfare. But in so doing, we do not accept their advice as always infallibly correct, since we realize that the judgments, points-of-view, and ability to foresee differ among the wise and experienced denizens of the spirit world as they do among those of this earth; however, we feel assured, from our own experiences in holding converse with spirits, that they are often better qualified to prophesy for us and have a keener insight into the future than our earthly friends, and thus are often in a better position to give us suggestions for our consideration in connection with our plans and conduct for the future.

If we do not possess the psychic power ourselves to communicate directly with spiritual beings, we must do the next best thing and find a medium whose psychic power or faculty is adapted to our purpose. We do the same in matters wholly of this world. When we seek advice from someone with whom we cannot directly communicate, we first satisfy ourselves as to that person's qualifications and then employ the best means of transmitting and retransmitting ideas between us.

It may be said that we may err in our selection of advisers, as well as in our means of intercommunication. And that is true, for we are not endowed with perfect judgment even in selecting in this life our medical or legal advisers, or our governmental representatives and officials, our business partners or our friends, or the persons to advise us as to where we can get the best advice in a given matter. And yet, the Spiritualist claims the right to act for himself without let or hindrance from those who differ from him in religious views. If he makes mistakes which cause him loss or suffering, it must be remembered that even Jesus, with his extraordinary psychic powers, made a mistake when he selected Judas Iscariot as one of the twelve. If it be said, that this seeming mistake was part of a divine plan, then it may be also said that the Spiritualist's seeming mistakes may also be a part of a divine plan.

Prophecy has been practiced for many centuries in connection with many religions. There have, of course, been false prophets as well as true prophets. But there are also good and bad men, honest and dishonest, false and fair, in every human calling. The existence of the false is no good or logical reason for attempting to hinder, stifle or destroy the true and honest. Because there are imposters and pseudo-mediums is no good reason for passing laws to silence the voice of honest mediums. The false and dishonest persons engaged in any legitimate work or business are only a small percentage of the whole number; and, therefore, it must appear an unwise policy, nay more, an unjust and oppressive procedure, to legislate the whole body out of their calling or employment because of the wrongs of the few. There are always weeds or tares among the wheat.

Spirit Manifestations of the Bible

From Genesis to Revelation, the nearness of the spirit world, and the intercommunication of spirits and mortals runs like a golden strand.

Not only spirit communion, but every phase of the manifestations distinctively known as Modern Spiritualism, is represented on many occasions, often hundreds of years apart. This similarity of expression shows that the same psychic laws held then as now, and there has been no change. Spiritualism furnishes the key whereby the mysteries of the Bible and its miracles are explained with a clearness commentators have not been able to attain for want of knowledge it furnishes. Though angels are understood to be special creations, and spirits to have ascended through mortal bodies, the words are used by the writers of the Bible as interchangeable as shown by the following passages:

"Yea, while I was speaking in prayer, even the man, Gabriel, whom I had seen in the vision." Dan. ix-21. He previously says that this spirit "stood before me as the appearance of a man." Chapter viii-15, "He maketh his angels spirits," Psalms, civ-4; Luke places departed spirits on a level with angels, xx-36: "Neither can they die any more, for they are equal unto the angels," etc.

The terms are indiscriminately used: "And as Peter knocked at the gate, a damsel came to harken—then said they it is his angel" (spirit). Acts xii-13,15: "I am he that liveth and was dead, and behold I am alive forever more." Rev. i-18: The soul of man separated from his body. Matt. xiv-26; Luke xxiv-37.

Spiritual Body

"There is a natural body and a spiritual body." I Cor. xv-44.

Physical Manifestations

The angel unloosed Peter from chains in prison:—"When they were past the first and second ward, they came to the iron gate that leadeth into the city, which opened to them of its own accord, and they went out." Acts xii-7-10.

"And when they came unto Lehi, the Philistines shouted against him, and the spirit of the Lord came mightily upon him, and the cords that were upon his arms became as flax that was

SPIRIT MANIFESTATIONS OF THE BIBLE 159

burnt with fire, and his bands loosed from off his hands." Jud. xv-14. A fine physical manifestation is recorded in Ex. xiv-25, where the Lord "Took off the chariot wheels" of the Egyptians. An angel went before them in a cloud. Ex. xiv-19. The moving of a table now, is paralleled by an angel rolling back the stone from the door of the sepulchre. Matt. xxviii-2.

Inspiration and Mediumship

"For to one is given by the spirit the word of wisdom; to another the word of knowledge by the same spirit." I Cor. xii-8. "And the spirit entered into me when he spake unto me, and set me upon my feet, that I heard him that spake unto me." Ezek. ii-2. "To whom has thou uttered words, and whose spirit came from thee?" Job xxvi-4.

Speaking Unknown Tongues

"To another divers kinds of tongues; to another the interpretation of tongues." I Cor. xii-10. "And they were filled with the Holy Ghost, and began to speak with other tongues, as the spirit (which controlled them) gave them utterance." Acts ii-4. "If any man speak in an unknown tongue, let it be by two or at most by three, and that by course, and let one interpret." I Cor. xiv-2, 27. If there was no interpreter they were to keep silent, for "the spirits of the prophets are subject to the prophets." It appears that they had a great deal of trouble in the meetings, or St. Paul would not have cautioned them to have all things "done decently and in order."

Materialization, and Clairvoyant Appearances

An angel appeared to Hagar, Gen. xvi; three came to Abraham so perfectly materialized, that "they did eat," Gen. xviii; and again to restrain him from sacrificing his son; to Lot, Chap. xix; an angel wrestled with Jacob, xxxii, 24; an angel spoke to all the people, Jud. ii; came and sat under an oak and talked to Gideon, Jud. vi; to Monoah, xii; the spirit of Samuel conversed with Saul, I Sam. xxviii; an angel came to feed Elijah, I Kings xix-5-8; protected the three Hebrew children from fire, Dan. iii. An angel appeared to Joseph in a dream, Matt. i; Moses and Elias appeared on the Mount; an angel appeared to the two Marys at the sepulchre;

to Zacharias, Luke i; to Mary, Luke i; to the shepherds, Luke ii; to Mary Magdalene, John xx; opened the prison doors, Acts v; to Cornelius, Acts x; to Peter in prison, Acts, xii; to Paul in "vision," Acts xvi and xxvii; and see Deut. iv-12. A "materialized" book was shown, Ezek. ii-9. Joshua saw and conversed with a spirit who held a drawn sword in his hand, Josh. v-13; and in Amos, it is said the "Lord stood upon a wall made by a plumb line with a plumb line in his hand." Samuel appeared "covered with a mantle." A spirit appeared to Daniel "clothed in linen, whose loins were girded with fine gold." Dan. x. Feeding the multitude of 5,000 on five loaves and two fishes. Luke ix, 12-17. Making wine at the marriage feast. John ii, 1-9. And lastly the several materializations of Christ after the crucifixion.

Trance

"How he was caught up into Paradise and heard unspeakable words which it is not lawful for man to utter." II Cor. xii-2, 4. Like all those who have fallen into trance, he did not know "whether in the body, or out of the body." "Which saw the vision of the Almighty, falling into a trance, but having his eyes open." Num. xxiv-16.

Ministry of Angels

"And the angels ministered unto him." Mark i-13. "And the angel of God called to Hagar out of heaven," when she was deserted in the wilderness. Gen. xxi-17. "The angels of the Lord encamp round about them that fear him, and delivereth them." Psalm xxxiv-7. "For he shall give his angels (spirits) charge over thee, to keep thee in all thy ways. They shall bear thee up in their hands, lest thou dash thy foot against a stone." Psalm xci-11, 12; Matt. xxvi-53; Acts v-18, 19, and viii-26 to 29. A man (spirit) appeared to Paul and said to him, "come over into Macedonia and help us." Acts xvi-9. "Are they not all ministering spirits, sent for to minister for them who shall be heirs to salvation?" Heb. i-14. Paul had a clear understanding of spiritual agencies. "Likewise the spirit also helpeth our infirmities." Rom. viii-26.

Direct Spirit Writing

On the walls of Babylon: "In the same hour came forth fingers of a man's hand, and wrote over against the candlestick upon the plaster of the wall of the king's palace, and the king saw the part of the hand that wrote." Dan. v-5.

David received the plan of the temple from a spirit: "And the pattern of all he had by the Spirit, of the courts of the house of the Lord." David gave to Solomon: I Chron. xxviii. The 19th verse says: "All this said David, the Lord made me understand in writing by his hand upon me, even all the work of this pattern."

"There came a writing to him (Jehoram) from Elijah the prophet." II Chron. xxi-12. According to the chronology, Elijah had been for some time dead, and hence it must have been by his spirit.

Levitation

"And when they were come up out of the water, the spirit of the Lord caught away Philip and the eunuch saw him no more —but Philip was found at Azotus." Acts viii-39, 40. The meaning intended, evidently is that Philip was transported by spirit power. This is clearly expressed in Ezek. iii-14. "So the spirit lifted me up and took me away." And more explicit, viii-3, "And he put forth the form of an hand, and took me by a lock of mine head; and the spirit lifted me up between the earth and the heaven, and brought me in the visions of God to Jerusalem, ⸺⸺." I Kings xviii-12. Elisha causes iron to swim. II Kings vi-6. Christ walked upon the sea. Mark vi-49.

Clairvoyance

"Come see a man who told me all things I ever did: Is not this the Christ?" John iv-16 to 29. Stephen, Acts vii-55, 56. "Behold I see the heavens opened and the son of man standing at the right hand of God." Paul was clairvoyant. Acts xxvii, Samuel is consulted as a seer by Saul. I Sam. ix-10 to 20.

Clairaudience

"And he fell to the earth, and heard a voice saying unto him: Saul, why persecutest thou me? And the men which journeyed with him stood speechless, hearing a voice but seeing no man." Acts ix-4, 7. The apostles heard the voices of Moses and Elias on the mount. Matt. xvii-3, 5; also Rev. i-10. "Now the Lord has told Samuel in his ear a day before Saul came." I Sam. ix-15, 16. Peter hears a spirit voice, Acts x-13. See Zech, i-9, 13; ii-2, 7; v-5-10; vi-4. Job is addressed by a spirit, iv-12 to 16.

Dreams and Visions

Often messages can be given during sleep that cannot be given during the more positive state of waking. "Then was the secret revealed to Daniel in a vision." Dan. ii-19. See Matt. i-20, ii-12; Acts ix-10, x-13; Gen. xv-12; xx-3, 7, xxxi-24, xii-7; Jud. vii-13; Num. xii-6; Deut. ii-1; iv-10, 18; Job. iv-13, vii-14, xxxii-8; I Sam. xxviii-6; Isa. xxix-8; Dan. ii-1, iv-18; Jer. xxvii; Joel ii-28; Eccl. v-3; I Cor. xiv-15. The entire Book of Revelation is professedly the utterance of one in trance.

Speaking Through Trumpets

Exo. xix-13, 16, 19; Rev. i-10.

Healing by Magnetised Articles or at a Distance

"Take my staff in thine hand and go thy way—and lay it on the face of the child." II Kings iv-29; Acts xix-12.

Healing

"They shall lay hands on the sick and they shall recover." Mark xvi-18. "And Jesus put forth his hand and touched him—and immediately his leprosy was cleansed." Matt. viii-3. Paul recovers his sight. Acts ix-17; Peter cures the lame man, Acts iii-1 to 8; Elisha restores the life of the Schunammite child." II Kings iv-33-35; the leper is cured, II Kings, v-10, 11; healing the damsel, Mark v-42. See Dan. x-18; Luke vii-21; viii-46; Mark v-30; vi-56; I Kings xvii-19-22; Math. x-1; Luke x-9; James v-14, 15. Jesus healed by magnetic touch: "and the whole multitude sought to touch him; for there went virtue out of him and healed them all." Luke vi-19.

Independent Spirit Voices

Deut. ix-12, 13; I Sam. iii-3, 9; Ezek. 1-28; Math. xvii-5; John xii-28-30; Acts vii-30-31, ix-4, 7; xi-7, 8, 9.

Lying Spirit

God used a lying spirit to persuade Ahab that he may go up and fall at Ramoth-gilead, I Kings xxii-19-23.

SPIRIT MANIFESTATIONS OF THE BIBLE 163

Bible References

The Old and the New Testament contain many passages showing that prophecy was a recognized spiritual gift and one that was sometimes falsely assumed or misused. A notable instance of false prophecy is recorded in I Kings, Chap. XXII, wherein it is said that God sent forth a spirit to be a lying spirit in the mouth of all of Ahab's prophets, for the purpose of persuading Ahab to go up to Ramoth-gilead, there to be killed in battle. Micaiah, true prophet, exposed this deception, and for his fidelity was put in prison and fed with the bread of affliction and with the water of affliction.

Spiritualists can not believe that the Infinite Spirit, whom men call God, could be a party to a false communication and no more can they believe that it was right to punish Micaiah.

Genesis

Chap. 16, 7th verse—The angel of the Lord appears to Hagar in the wilderness and comforts her.

Chap. 18, 2 to 8 verse—The angel of the Lord (as three men) appear to Abraham.

Chap. 19, 1st verse—Two angels (previously referred to as men) appear to Lot, and warn him to flee.

Chap. 28, 11-12 verses—Jacob's vision of an angel ascending and descending.

Chap. 32, 1-2 verses—Angels meet Jacob.

Chap. 15, 12 verse—Abraham goes in trance.

Chap. 16, 7 verse—Angel of Lord appears to Hagar.

Chap. 24, 7 verse—The Lord sends his angel before Abraham's servant to help him select wife for Isaac.

Exodus

Chap. 3, 2 verse—Angels speak to Moses out of the burning bush.

Chap. 19, 16-19 verse—The Lord speaks to Moses through the trumpet. Moses spake and God answered him by a voice.

Chap. 23, 20-23 verse—The Lord promises Moses an angel for a guide.

Numbers

Chap. 9, 15-23 verse—The Lord guides the Israelites by a cloud, covering the tabernacle by day, and a pillar of fire by night.

Chap. 11, 25 verse—The Lord came down in a cloud and spake with Moses, took the spirit upon him and caused the seventy to prophesy.

Chap. 22, 23 verse—An angel appears to Balaam's Ass; 31 verse, opens Balaam's eyes and he sees an angel.

Joshua, Chap. 5, 13-15 verse—Captain of the Hosts of the Lord appears to Joshua.

Judges, Chap. 6, 11 verse—An angel appears to Gideon and sits and talks with him.

Samuel, Chap. 28, 12 verse—Samuel appears to the woman of Endor, and talks with Saul.

Kings, Chap. 19, 5-8 verse—Angel touches, talks with, and feeds Elijah.

Ezekiel, Chap. 2, 2 verse—Spirit entrances Ezekiel.

Daniel, Chap. 3-24 verse—Angel protects three men in fiery furnace.

Daniel, Chap. 5, 5 verse—The handwriting on the wall at Belshazzar's feast.

Daniel, Chap. 10, 21-22 verse—A man (spirit) appears, Gabriel appears and talks with Daniel.

And it came to pass, that, when the spirit rested upon them, they prophesied, and did not cease.

Numbers C. XI, v. 25.

From the 27th, 28th and 29th verses of the 11th chapter of Numbers, we learn that two men upon whom the spirit rested, went not out unto the tabernacle, but prophesied in the camp, and thereby aroused some envious opposition. They did not exercise their spiritual gifts in the "holy place," but were satisfied to do so among the people in the camp. This seems to have been their offense. Parallels can be found in this day. Mediums who prophesy, comfort, warn and encourage, in the sanctity of their homes, are stamped as fortunetellers and declared to be, by some of our laws, vagrants, vagabonds and disorderly persons, but when these same things are done in churches and temples, a divine atmosphere, like that of the tabernacle, is supposed to attach to the prophets or mediums and sanctify their utterances. How Moses disposed of the matter we gather from the following:

27. And there ran a young man, and told Moses, and said, Eldad and Medad do prophesy in the camp.

28. And Joshua, the son of Nun, the servant of Moses, one of his young men answered and said MY LORD, MOSES, FORBID THEM.

29. And Moses said unto him, Enviest thou for my sake? WOULD GOD THAT ALL THE LORD'S PEOPLE WERE PROPHETS, and that the Lord would put his spirit upon them.

And he said, Hear now my words: If there be a PROPHET among you, I the Lord will make myself known unto him in a vision, and will speak unto him in a dream.
Numbers C. XII, v. 6.

Deborah, a PROPHETESS, the wife of Lapidoth, she judged Israel.
Judges C, IV, v. 4.

Miriam, the sister of Aaron, was a PROPHETESS.
Exodus, C. XV. v. 20.

Woe unto the foolish prophets, THAT FOLLOW THEIR OWN SPIRIT, AND HAVE SEEN NOTHING.
Ezekiel, C. XIII, v. 3.

Elisha, the prophet, that is in Israel telleth the King of Israel THE WORDS THAT THOU SPEAKEST IN THY BEDCHAMBER.
II King, C. VI, v. 12.

When Hilkiah, the high priest, told Shaphan, the scribe, that he had found the book of the law (which according to biblical students had been lost for a thousand years), and Shaphan took it to the king, "the king commanded them to enquire of the Lord concerning the words of this book." What did they do? They went to a medium, a prophetess; and it is written:

So Hilkiah, the priest, and Ahikham and Achor, and Shaphan, and Asahiah, went unto Hulda, the prophetess, the wife of Shallukm, the son of Tikvah, the son of Harhas, keeper of the wardrobe: (now she dwelt in Jerusalem in the college); AND THEY COMMUNED WITH HER.
II Kings, C. XXII, v. 8 to 14.

Here follows an appeal from the prophet which does not appear to have been directed altogether to the spiritual nature of those to whom the message was given:

And the spirit of God came upon Zechariah the son of Jehoiada the priest, which stood above the people, and he said unto them, Thus saith God, Why transgress ye the commandments of the LORD, THAT YE CANNOT PROSPER? because ye have forsaken the Lord, he hath also forsaken you.

II Chronicles, C. XXIV, v. 20.

That the services of the seer were not always appreciated may be gathered from the following communication, for the delivery of which the seer was thrown into prison:

And at that time Hanani THE SEER came to Asa, king of Judah, and said unto him, Because thou hast relied on the king of Syria, and not relied on the Lord thy God, therefore is the host of the king of Syria escaped out of thine hand.

II Chronicles, C. XVI, v. 7 to 10.

The spirit of Samuel, by an independent voice, prophesied to Saul the fate of himself and his sons at the time that Saul paid the visit to the medium of Endor:

Moreover the Lord will also deliver Israel with thee into the hand of the Philistines; AND TO-MORROW SHALL THOU AND THY SONS BE WITH ME: the Lord also shall deliver the host of Israel in to the hand of the Philistines.

I Samuel, C, XXVIII, v. 19.

The verification of this prophecy or prediction is found in I Samuel, C. XXXI.

Saul himself appears to have been chosen as one of the prophets, and yet he seems to have been unable to get a message from the spirit world for himself; and so, in his extremity, he sought a medium, even though he had previously decreed the death of all mediums.

I Samuel, C. X, v. 7, also C. XXVIII.

Saul's father had lost some asses and he with a servant was sent in search of them. After a fruitless effort to find them, Saul was about to return, but the servant told him there was in the city a man of God, an honorable man; and that all he said surely came to pass; and he advised consulting this man. I Samuel C. IX. From this chapter it seems clear that it was the custom to consult men of God in regard to lost property and to pay them for their services;

and that a man of God was simply a seer, and that in this case Samuel foretold the finding of the asses:

7. Then said Saul to his servant, But, behold, if we go, WHAT SHALL WE BRING THE MAN? For the bread is spent in our vessels, and there is not a present to bring to the man of God: What have we?

8. And the servant answered Saul again, and said, Behold, I HAVE HERE AT HAND THE FOURTH PART OF A SHEKEL OF SILVER; THAT WILL I GIVE THE MAN OF GOD, TO TELL US OUR WAY.

9. Before time in Israel, WHEN A MAN WENT TO INQUIRE OF GOD THUS HE SPAKE, COME, LET US GO TO THE SEER FOR HE THAT IS NOW CALLED A PROPHET WAS BEFORE TIME CALLED A SEER.)

19. And Samuel answered Saul, and said I AM THE SEER; go up before me unto the high place; for ye shall eat with me today, and tomorrow I will let thee go, AND WILL TELL THEE ALL THAT IS IN THINE HEART.

20. And as for thine asses that were lost three days ago, set not thy mind on them; for they are found.

New Testament References

Matthew

Chap. 1, 20 verse—An angel appears to Joseph.

Chap. 2, 13 verse—Angel warns Joseph to flee into Egypt.

Chap. 3, 16-17 verse—Jesus sees the Spirit of God descending like a dove.

Chap. 17, 1-8 verse—Moses and Elias appear to Jesus, Peter, James and John.

Chap. 28, 9 verse—Jesus appears to Mary Magdalene and the other Mary.

Luke, Chap. 2, 25-27 verse—Simeon led by a spirit.

Acts

Chap. 2, 1 verse—The Disciples speak in divers tongues.

Chap. 4, 13 verse—Peter and John speak filled with the holy Spirit.

Chap. 5, 1 verse—Peter psychically proves Ananias guilty of cheating.

Chap. 5, 19 verse—Angel opens prison doors.

Chap. 8, 29 verse—Spirit (called a man) bids Philip go after rich man's chariot.

Chap. 9, 3-7 verse—Jesus speaks with Paul.

Chap. 9, 10 verse—Jesus speaks to Ananias and tells him to go and meet Paul.

Chap. 10, 10 verse—Paul falls into a trance.

Chap. 12, 7 verse—Angel releases Peter from prison.

Chap. 27, 22 verse—Angel warns Paul of shipwreck.

Quench not the spirit, despise not PROPHESYINGS.

I Thessalonians, C. V. v. 19 and 20.

But it is NOT YE THAT SPEAK, BUT THE SPIRIT of your Father which speaketh in you.

Matthew, C. X., v. 20.

Philip, the evangelist, had four virgin daughters who did PROPHESY.

Acts, C. XXI, v. 8 and 9.

---

4. Now there are DIVERSITIES OF GIFTS, but the same Spirit.

5. And there are differences of administrations, but the same Lord.

6. And there are diversities of operations, but it is the same God which worketh all in all.

7. But the manifestation of the Spirit is given to every man to profit withal.

8. For to one is given by the Spirit the word of wisdom; to another the word of knowledge by the same Spirit.

9. To another faith by the same Spirit; to another the gifts of healing by the same Spirit.

10. To another the working of miracles; TO ANOTHER PROPHECY; to another discerning of Spirits; to another divers kinds of tongues; to another the interpretation of tongues.

11. But all these worketh that one and the selfsame Spirit, DIVIDING TO EVERY MAN SEVERALLY AS HE WILL.

I Corinthians, C. XII, v. 4 to 12.

And God hath set some in the church, first apostles SECONDARILY PROPHETS, thirdly teachers, after that miracles, then gifts of healing, etc.

I Corinthians, C. XII, v. 28.

SPIRIT MANIFESTATIONS OF THE BIBLE 169

Follow after charity, and desire spiritual gifts, BUT RATHER THAT YE MAY PROPHESY.

I Corinthians, C. XIV, v. 1.

But he that PROPHESIETH speaketh unto men to EDIFICATION, AND EXHORTATION, AND COMFORT.

I Corinthians, C. XIV, v. 3.

---

31. For ye may PROPHESY one by one, that all may learn and all may be comforted.

32. And the Spirits of the PROPHETS are subject to the PROPHETS.

39. Wherefore, brethren, COVET TO PROPHESY, and forbid not to speak with tongues.

I Corinthians, C. XIV, v. 31, 32 and 39.

Religious Liberty and the Law

Contrary to the religious liberty vouchsafed to the people by the Federal Constitution and the Constitutions of the various States, persecution under guise of the exercise of the police power of the State, has been visited upon the heads of spiritual mediums, connected with and working for the religion of Spiritualism. It is not competent for any State to enlarge, by statute, the police power and thereby restrict the rights and privileges which the people have been exercising under a higher law. It is a strange spectacle to see legislatures, the great majority of whose membership are believers in the New Testament, seeking by statute to prevent prophesying by those upon whom the spirit rests, while Paul, in his epistles, urged the early Christians not to despise prophesying, but to covet it.

If the law can prevent mediums from prophesying as to past or future events, then it can also prevent priests and preachers from foretelling what the future life of saints and sinners will be. Real prophecy now scarcely exists in the so-called orthodox churches; the spiritual gifts of which Paul writes so forcibly have almost entirely faded away from Christianity and have found a new expression in the Gospel of Spiritualism. The letter killeth but the spirit giveth life.

It is sometimes asserted that it is improper for mediums to take fees for their services. But do not the ministers of all religions receive compensation, in some form or other, for their services? As long as mediums are living in this material world, they are obliged to meet the costs of living, like all other human beings, no matter how spiritual their work or they themselves may be. If the law can forbid mediums to take fees for their spiritual communications, then it can also forbid the priest to take money for saying prayers for the dead. Such money is given and received with the mutual understanding that prayers said for souls in purgatory by a priest of the church, helps those souls to be relieved from effects of their sins. The church does not pretend to prove this a fact; it is merely a theological assumption, a dogma, a matter of faith. Men and angels know that the good and true mediums do not, as a rule, have much of this world's goods; and that many mediums beside being poor, are compelled to bear the contumely of thoughtless and vicious people, and also suffer many things, which are placed upon them from the spirit side by the lower elements.

If mediums sometimes make mistakes or messages do not always come through them with accuracy, we must remember that all human agencies sometimes err and that even spirits that communicate with us do not claim perfection.

It is, to say the least, a dangerous thing, for the State to make the doing of a thing for money, a crime; when the doing of that thing without money is in no-wise criminal. The full extent to which the law should go in limiting religious freedom, is to prevent fraud, immorality, and traitorous conduct and doctrines. Upon these points we will stand with the State, but the attempt to throttle legitimate mediumship and to hush the voice of prophesy will fail in this age, as it has failed before; for, being of God, man cannot destroy them.

(C. R. Schirm.)

Spiritualist Progressive Lyceum

The Spiritualist Progressive Lyceum was founded at a meeting held at Dodsworth Hall, No. 806 Broadway, New York City, by Andrew Jackson Davis, on January 25, 1863.

In his remarks during the course of the meeting, Mr. Davis said:

"We have assembled this afternoon to inaugurate an association for the physical and spiritual improvement of both sexes and of all ages.

"The plan is not original with me. It is an attempt to unfold and actualize on earth, partially at least, a progressive juvenile assemblage like those in the summer land, whither children are constantly going from earth, and where they are received into groups for improvement, growth and graduation.

Thus the idea of the LYCEUM was based upon a vision of the great association of Lyceums existing in the Spirit World, as seen in vision by this great seer, which he describes as "one of the most classical, progressive and musical brotherhoods in the homeland of the Good, the True and the Beautiful."

Andrew Jackson Davis was one of the great psychics and seers of the ages, lecturing at an early age before educated and enlightened men and societies, and writing during his life time many of the books of the deepest and most profound philosophy, and of the science of life as it is manifested in the Spirit World.

He was so sensitive that he could remember his spiritual wanderings in the spirit world and on awakening to physical consciousness gave vivid and beautiful descriptions of conditions existing there.

Among other things he has stated that he saw, "Children continually passing from their homes on earth into their homes in the spirit world." "Being received into beautiful homes and cared for and nursed by good wise men and loving women in the summer land." He saw "Children at their play and at their lessons; on their visits to other societies of children, and taking part in music, in singing and in their beautiful marches."

Quoting from "Outlines of Spiritualism for the Young" by Alfred Kitson, "Mr. Davis saw that the children when met in Sessions in their Lyceums were arranged in 'groups,' all the members of one group being of similar age. Then these groups were named by their Spirit Leaders as they thought would best express their nature and the unfoldment of their powers."

He was so pleased with all the things he saw that it filled him with a desire to have similar schools on earth where people could be taught how to grow to be wise and good and true, with a correct understanding of their own bodies and of their own souls as well as of a knowledge of the true conditions existing in the Spirit World, and of the effect the lives lived on the earth plane will have upon the condition of the soul as it enters the Spirit World.

Organizing a Lyceum

The manner of organizing and conducting a Lyceum varies in different localities according to conditions prevailing, the number of Lyceumists attending and the ages of those who do attend.

A good general form which is elastic and can be varied to meet the needs of the occasion may be outlined about as follows:

Seats should be provided in advance and placed in different parts of the hall, or meeting room, in circle or class form, sufficient to seat all who will attend the different classes arranged for.

Lyceums should always start promptly at hour and moment announced, even if there are only two or three present, and should be closed as punctually at the usual closing time.

Each member should be present and in their seats at the time set for the opening of the Lyceum meeting.

At the time announced, Lyceum Leader sounds bell, All rise: Sing two verses of hymn previously selected. Invocation by member of Lyceum, Remain standing:—Give pledge to flag.

> "I Pledge allegiance to the Flag of the
> United States of America and to the
> Republic for which it stands, one nation under God,
> Indivisible, with liberty and justice for all.

Give the Flag Salute, By C. Fannie Allyn:
> "Hail Star Spangled Banner, the sign of the free,
> Our hearts and our hands pledge allegiance to thee,
> We salute thee and echo from shore unto shore
> One country united, one flag evermore."

Still standing, repeat the "DECLARATION OF PRINCI-

PLES," as adopted by the National Spiritualist Association of Churches, in unison with, or following the Lyceum Leader.

At sound of bell all be seated, class conference, on topic selected on previous Sunday, the leader of each class encouraging each member to express their views, and to ask questions on subject under consideration.

Above takes about forty-minutes.

At sound of bell classes all rise and form for marching and physical exercises, lasting about fifteen minutes.

At sound of bell all resume seats.

Leader of the Lyceum then asks members of each class to give their thoughts to the Lyceum, upon the subject that has been considered in their class, asking the leader of the class last for her views upon the question. Care should be taken not to embarrass any of the class members by insisting on extended statements or explanations. Often members of classes will merely state the subject of conference without expressing individual views, but will gradually be led into a more free expression of thought, by patience, consideration, and encouragement.

Offertory.

Announcements by leader of each class of subject selected for conference on following Sunday.

Memory Gems.

Songs.

Short recitations by those willing to give them.

Closing hymn.

Benediction.

Invitation to come again.

Lyceum meetings should last about one hour and a half and be kept interesting all the time.

Before the physical exercises a popular or patriotic song may be sung, all joining in the singing.

Chidren should hold office when possible and should be invited in turn to offer invocation, benediction, to take up offertory, distribute and collect banners, care for books and any other duties connected with the conduct of the Lyceum. Nothing holds the interest of the children or other members so effectively as to feel that they are taking an active and useful part in the conducting of the Lyceum.

The Lyceum should elect its conductor, but it is sometimes found advisable for the conductor to appoint the other officers, or leaders, those being Class Leaders, Secretary, Treasurer, Collector, Chaplain, Librarian, and other officers that may be found advisable.

There can be no more important or valuable work done for the cause of Spiritualism than in the founding and the maintaining of Lyceums.

Every Church and Society should have its Lyceum, and yet the founding of Lyceums is not dependent upon Church or Society, but often may be started in localities or communities where no other society exists.

A Lyceum may be started in the home where there are father, mother, perhaps two children, with two or three young cousins from down the street and perhaps one or two neighbors from next door.

A song may be sung and invocation offered, and a page or two read from some good suitable Spiritualist book of which there are many, and then conference and discussion upon the article read out of the book.

As these meetings continue, interest will grow and from small beginnings, strong societies may be formed, but the Lyceum should always be continued and interest in its work maintained.

The object of the Lyceum is, not to teach the individual, whether child or adult, to accept and memorize ideas, theories or answers to questions that have been formulated by others, but is rather to teach them to think for themselves and to develop their own ideas in regard to all things affecting their own relationship to the universe and to God, their own welfare and happiness, their own growth and unfoldment physically, mentally and spiritually, on this material plane of life, also in the Spirit World.

Investigation, study and conference of this kind will gradually but surely bring to each one the full realization that all the manifestations of nature, whether in the vegetable, animal, mental, or spiritual kingdom are subject to immutable and unchangeable law, and what a man wishes himself, or his life to be, he must make for himself by an understanding of and compliance with the laws of nature, which are the laws of God.

The soul grows even as the mighty oak grows and only by living in accordance with spiritual law can spiritual development be attained.

The Declaration of Principles adopted by the National Spiritualist Association of Churches, also the Spiritualist definition of the four words, Spiritualism, Spiritualist, Medium, Healer, should be carefully read over, analyzed, criticized and otherwise discussed until each one feels satisfied that he thoroughly understands them, and after that they may profitably be perfectly memorized.

In these pages will be found a list of Questions and Answers about Spiritualism. We do not recommend memorizing them, at any time. They are offered only as seed thoughts from which may be derived useful and desirable subjects for consideration and for conference, and in such conference much more logical and satisfactory answers to the questions may be developed and a clearer understanding obtained by the members of the class. Valuable lessons may also be obtained from a consideration of the Bible References to be found on other pages of this Manual, also from "SELECTED QUOTATIONS" on still other pages.

As a study of the laws of nature and of the philosophy of Spiritualism continue, the interest of the members of the class will continue to grow and expand, for everywhere in nature it will be found that all of the laws of nature blend in perfect harmony and unity, and that the desired and desirable is obtained, not by miracle, or by prayer for special interposition of divine providence, but by an understanding of and compliance with the laws of nature, which are the laws of God, by which and through which alone, Spirit comes in contact with and manifests upon, the material, the mental, and the spiritual realms of life.

"Spiritualism Is a Science" because it investigates, analyzes and classifies facts and manifestations, demonstrated from the spirit side of life.

"Spiritualism Is a Philosophy" because it studies the laws of nature both on the seen and unseen sides of life and bases its conclusions upon present observed facts. It accepts statements of observed facts of past ages and conclusions drawn therefrom, when sustained by reason and by results of observed facts of the present day.

"Spiritualism Is a Religion" because it strives to understand and to comply with the Physical, Mental and Spiritual Laws of Nature, "which are the laws of God."

Much beautiful spiritual inspiration, from which topics for class consideration may be gathered, will be found in many of the poems

SPIRITUALIST PROGRESSIVE LYCEUM

which are printed on the closing pages of this Manual. Valuable lessons may also be found in the chapter under the heading "Philosophy of Spiritualism," also in the chapters "Selected Quotations," "The Spirit of World," "Questions and Anwers About Spiritualism," "Bible References" and "Suggestions for Self Culture."

It will be found helpful and profitable to all who wish to acquire a broader knowledge of Spiritualism to take up the correspondence courses of study, upon the Science, Philosophy and Religion of Spiritualism, as prepared and published by the Bureau of Education of the National Spiritualist Association of Churches. The name and address of the superintendent and of the secretary of the Bureau of Education will be found in the current issue of the N. S. A. C. Year Book, or in the current issue of "THE NATIONAL SPIRITUALIST."

Questions and Answers About Spiritualism

What Is a Spiritualist?

A Spiritualist is one who believes, as the basis of his or her religion, in the communication between this and the spirit world by means of mediumship, and who endeavors to mould his or her character and conduct in accordance with the highest teachings derived from such communication.

Can a Spiritualist Accept the Teaching of Jesus?

Yes. A belief in spirit communication does not conflict with the Teachings ascribed to Jesus. The Christian Bible confirms its truth repeatedly.

Is Spiritualism a Religion?

It is a Religion, Philosophy and Science in one. It has a National Organization, State Associations, numbers of churches, and a solemnly ordained ministry.

What Should Convince Me of Its Truths?

Your own reason and common sense after a thorough and scientific investigation.

How Should I Go About This Investigation?

By obtaining literature from the National Spiritualist Association of Churches and by questioning the officials of State Associations or pastors of local churches. Study the Philosophy of Spiritualism and the Phenomena which demonstrates and proves its Philosophy.

How Can I Study the Philosophy?

By carefully reading and thinking over the literature mentioned, and by taking the trouble to ask questions of our officials and others qualified to answer.

How Can I Study the Phenomena?

By attending services held by local Spiritualist Churches, at which these phenomena are actually demonstrated by our mediums.

QUESTIONS AND ANSWERS ABOUT SPIRITUALISM

What Is a Medium?

A Medium is one whose organism is sensitive to vibrations from the spirit world, and through whose instrumentality, intelligences in that world are able to convey messages and produce the phenomena of Spiritualism.

What Is This Influence?

It is the transference of impressions or ideas by a disembodied spirit direct to the brain of the Medium. The most noted scientists of today recognize that thought transference is possible and call it "Telepathy."

How Do You Know This Influence Is Exercised by Spirits?

Because under it Mediums accomplish things which would be impossible to them under ordinary conditions and plainly show in many other ways that they are being used as a medium of communication by some other individual.

Then Are These Mediums "Fortune-Tellers?"

No! Our mediums, many of whom are ordained clergy of our church, thus perform a sacred duty. Communications coming through them, frequently refer to material and everyday matters because you ask for such, and because, to a certain extent, such are necessary to arouse interest and induce further investigation.

But Do They Not Foretell the Future?

It is sometimes done to a certain extent through their means. An inhabitant of the Spirit World can, to a degree, predict future events with greater or less accuracy, according to conditions. This is done by *reasoning* based on observation of past and present conditions and events, and is more accurate than is the same process as used by us, because the Spirit reasoner is not hampered by a physical body, nor by the conventional and set ideas that go with the limitations of such a body.

Then of What Use Is Spiritualism, If Not to Predict the Future?

This is a mistaken idea held by many people. The prediction of the future is of very little importance. Spiritualism's greatest value lies in the fact that, when its truth is generally accepted, it will completely revolutionize many accepted but antiquated ideas and customs.

In What Way Could That Be Possible?

Because Spiritualism proves not only that we continue to exist consciously after the death of the physical body, but that we are then still responsible for our actions while here. We cannot escape the consequences of our acts, good or bad. Therefore, if a majority of earth's inhabitants become firmly convinced of this fact, plainly the glaring defects and abuses of our present life will gradually disappear, as each individual will exercise greater care not to injure others, because of the consequences and resultant injuries to himself.

Is Spirit Communication Necessary to Bring This About?

Yes! Because that is the only *definite* and *positive* way by which the fact of *unavoidable personal responsibility after "death"* can be unalterably proven to man. All present-day religions teach this to a certain degree, but all absolutely fail to convince their followers *beyond doubt*, because they must rely on faith alone and cannot give definite proof.

What Other Benefit Is Spirit Communication?

It completely removes the fear of death, by proving that there is no death of the actual person. It convinces us that it is merely stepping from a lower state of existence into a higher, exactly as the worm apparently "dies" to become the butterfly. It does away with absolute separation of those closely united, thereby relieving us of the worst of material sorrows. It also inspires us to purer and more progressive ways of life, by proving beyond doubt the advantages of right action and the disadvantages of wrong action.

Why Do Your Mediums Not Confine Themselves to This Teaching, Instead of Giving the Messages We Generally Hear?

Because, like a baby, the average person must creep before he can walk—that is, he must first become interested in investigating, then become thoroughly convinced that the manifestations are caused by his friends in Spirit Life and then he may begin to study the philosophy. These questions and answers are designed to be a groundwork in such investigations and study, exactly as one must learn to read before he can study the higher sciences.

But Why Do Mediums Accept Fees for Their Work?

For the same reason that ministers and priests accept fees for weddings, baptisms, funerals, etc., in addition to their regular salaries. They are special, personal services, for which the clergyman is entitled to a special and personal fee for his knowledge and time.

Why Was Spirit Communication Not Established Long Ago?

Because at no time in history have the people at large been ready to receive it, until now. Spirit communications have been constantly given during thousands of years, but only the priesthood of each nation were sufficiently educated to recognize and receive them. The people were densely ignorant and grossly material in thought, and therefore could understand only material things, and so left no way open for spirit communications to be understood.

Then Must We Be Highly Educated to Receive Spirit Communications Direct?

No, but you must remember that the least educated American citizen is far more enlightened than were the common people of even a century ago. There must be at least some ground work of education and the right to free thought, in order to remove superstition and lay a foundation for the proper understanding of spiritual manifestations.

But Some of Your Mediums Seem to Have Little Education?

That is one convincing proof. We often receive, through mediums of a moderate education, communications which plainly come from a trained and educated mind. That alone is strong evidence that the message does not originate with the mediums, but comes from without.

Some Manifestations Seem Childish, of What Use Are "Rapings," and the Like?

Such conclusions are not the result of careful thought; as the rappings of a telegraph instrument, when properly interpreted, carry messages of vital import from nation to nation and around the world, so rappings from spirit world, when properly interpreted, carry messages of vital import and of highest philosophy from the inhabitants of the spirit world to man on the earth plane, by the use of natural forces.

To What "Natural Forces" Do You Refer?

Electric currents, the same as are used in operating the telegraph instrument, also as now used in sending the wireless message from city to city and from continent to continent. It is no more logical to call the spirit rap childish than it would be to call the dot and dash of the telegraph childish. As the telegraph instrument is only a toy to a child, so the rap from the spirit world seems only a toy to the uninformed mind that fails to grasp the vast import of the fact that there is no death, and that definite communication has at least been established between man in the mortal and man in the spirit body.

Are You Willing to Submit to Scientific Investigation?

Certainly. We court scientific and philosophical investigation of our phenomena and philosophy.

Then Why Has Not Science Demonstrated Your Claims?

Every scientist who has investigated thoroughly and without prejudice has been convinced of the truth of these facts. Some of the greatest minds of our day, such as Sir Arthur Conan Doyle, Alfred Russell Wallace, Sir William Crookes (discoverer of the x-ray), Camille Flammarion, William T. Stead and Sir Oliver Lodge of England, Edgar Lucien Larkin, of Mt. Lowe Observatory, and other world-famous scientific men have announced themselves convinced.

Then Why Do Scientists Reject These So-Called Facts?

Some men are so prejudiced that they make no investigations. Others investigate unfairly, demanding material proof of spiritual truths without being willing to assist in forming the spiritual conditions necessary to produce the results desired, which is unfair and as impossible as it would be to carry an electrical message from one city to another on a silk thread or a ball of twine.

Why Do You Not Attempt to Convince the Scientific World?

Unprejudiced scientists have found no difficulty in finding

absolute scientific proof of the possibility of communicating with the spirit people, under proper conditions.

Would Your Beliefs, if Accepted, Upset Modern Science?

No. Spiritualism is the only religion which harmonizes with science in every way. Not one proven scientific fact contradicts the truths we teach, but on the other hand, all uphold and prove our conclusions.

Why Then Do We Not Hear More Scientific Teachings From Your Platforms?

Because our teachings must be so explained as to be understood by all minds. Many people can be interested only by tests or messages dealing with material matters. Also we find it necessary to prove our phenomena, before we can interest the public in our philosophy. Very few people accept as a fact the possibility of the continuity of life.

Does the Exercise of Mediumship Harm the Medium?

No more than any other work. In fact, it is distinctly beneficial if combined with proper exercise, relaxation, and recreation, which everybody should have. Some Mediums have an inclination to overwork and are then harmed just as anyone would be who carried any occupation to excess. We know of many cases in which Mediums have been benefited physically and mentally, by their work, to an astonishing extent.

Are Spirit Communications Always Correct?

Not always but usually so. The spirit merely uses its best judgment in offering advice, and although it can see many causes which produce certain results, more clearly than the average mortal can do, they are still fallible, and so claim to be, and are liable at times to be mistaken. It is also true that there are times, when owing to certain physical conditions or weaknesses, the Medium cannot be reached by the particular spirit who would be best able to give the advice desired. A Medium acting wisely under such conditions would refrain from exercising her mediumship until more perfect mental and physical conditions should obtain. We claim not that our sensitives are infallible but that they are honestly doing their best to help you, and that they DO bring messages from the spirit world.

Are There Other Methods of Communication Besides Spirit Raps?

Yes; since the knowledge of spirit communication came to be understood by the human mind much of bigotry, superstition, and prejudice have been removed, and the human organism has been able to respond to natural impulses without fear of persecution and possible death. As a result we find mediumship manifesting in many beautiful forms, such as those of clairvoyance, clairaudience, slate writing, materialization, spirit healing and inspiration.

How Can I Know That Any Particular Medium Is Trustworthy?

Most mediums are honest in their intentions, but none can ever claim to be infallible. Such a claim on their part would of itself be a positive proof of their lack of knowledge and honesty, and would prove them unworthy of confidence. The mistrust, by the public, of mediums and mediumship, is the result largely of ignorance, or superstition on the part of some who have not learned to understand that messages from the Spirit world are natural and do not claim to be supernatural or infallible.

Is Not Mediumship a Supernatural Gift?

No. Mediumship is a natural gift, and is subject to the operation of natural laws, as are all the manifestations of nature whether in the material or the spiritual world, which must be understood and complied with.

Is There Any Way of Knowing Who Are the Recognized Mediums in the Spiritualist Ranks?

Yes. The National and State Spiritualist Associations issue certificates each year to mediums whom they believe to be qualified and worthy.

Can Any One Get These Certificates?

We grant such certificates only after the applicant has undergone certain educational training and examination and has proven himself competent to receive and transmit communications from the Spirit World. Our Mediums correspond to

QUESTIONS AND ANSWERS ABOUT SPIRITUALISM

the clergy of denominational churches. We have Ordained Ministers, Licentiates, Certified Mediums, and Healers.

Can I Depend Upon Getting a Satisfactory Spirit Communication Through Any Medium Holding Such Certificates?

Not necessarily so. Not even our best developed mediums can reach into all conditions satisfactorily for all people; some can receive messages for one individual and others for another. There are conditions and laws governing mediumship which are not generally understood but which must be complied with in order to obtain satisfactory results.

What Class of Spirits May One Expect to Come in Contact with When Visiting a Spiritualist Medium?

The character of the spirits one will meet in visiting a Medium is liable to be as varied as are those of the individuals one comes in contact with each day on the earth plane.

Can You Classify Them According to Their Desires and Intentions?

Each Spirit communicating through a Medium does so with a special object in view. In a general way they may be classified under three different heads. FIRST, those who are so bound to earth conditions that they will try to come in contact, and communicate with it through any avenue they find available. SECOND, those who are naturally attracted to us by the ties of relationship and the laws of love. THIRD, those advanced and developed Spirits who return from the higher spheres of life in the Spirit world, filled with a Holy Love for Humanity, for the purpose of guiding and leading mankind into higher knowledge and further light.

Do Not Messages Sometimes Come from Spirits Who Have Never Lived in a Physical Body?

We have no knowledge of any such Spirits. Those returning even from the higher spheres of spirit life all claim to have traveled this way, to have met and overcome temptations, to have unfolded a knowledge of God's laws which are nature's laws both on the material and on the spiritual sides of life, and to have earned by honest work and effort their right to the light which they have attained.

Do You Not Often Come in Contact with Evil Spirits?

Those whom you call evil spirits are also the spirits of those who have lived on the earth plane. Many of them through lack of opportunity, want of proper education, and the influence of wrong social conditions have passed through this world and into the Spirit World in absolute ignorance of spiritual laws. They are, however, no worse than mankind has sent them into the Spirit World, and they are still our Brothers and Sisters.

Are You Not Afraid to Come in Contact with Such Spirits?

No. It is no more dangerous to come in contact with the undeveloped in the Spirit World than it is to come in contact with the undeveloped on the material plane of life. Ignorance of the presence of an undeveloped spirit is no safeguard against its influence upon the individual with whom it comes in contact. Only by a knowledge of these laws will mankind ever be able to free itself from undesirable conditions which sometimes cause insanity, drunkenness, murder, suicide and war.

Will a Knowledge of Spiritualism Produce These Results?

Yes. What ignorance and superstition have failed to do, a knowledge of Nature's laws can accomplish. The TRUTH alone can free the Human mind and start it on the pathway in search of truth, physical, mental and spiritual truth.

What Effect Does the Fact of Spirit Communication Have on the Undeveloped Spirits?

The spirits from the darker spheres often are allowed to visit the Spiritualist circle, in order that they may obtain a knowledge of things which were denied them while they were on earth. Oftentimes they come honestly seeking for knowledge and for light. Such spirits on learning for the first time that there is still an opportunity for them to develop and to outgrow the unhappy conditions acquired during their life on earth, seek earnestly to unfold into better conditions. They return frequently to the circle seeking more light, and in time they start on their pathway of eternal progression. Thus by showing the light in all dark places on both sides of life, by educating both man in the body and man in the spirit will our earth be freed from that darkness which man calls evil.

QUESTIONS AND ANSWERS ABOUT SPIRITUALISM 187

Will All Then Have An Opportunity to Progress, and to Undo the Many Mistakes Committed on This Side of Life?

Yes. Every human soul born into life is a child of GOD and the opportunity for development will at some time be realized and taken advantage of by each one. Spiritualism proclaims "The doorway to reformation is never closed against any human soul here or hereafter."

What Other Principles Does Spiritualism Proclaim and Uphold?

The National Spiritualist Association of Churches, of the United States of America has adopted what is known as its "Declaration of Principles" which consists of nine short articles.

All of the nine Declaration of Principles will be found printed on Page 34 of this Manual.

Do You Believe in "Good" and "Evil" Spirits?

We believe there are both intelligent and ignorant spirits. No being is naturally "bad"—evil always originates in ignorance. Merely leaving the physical body does not change the condition of the spirit, which is the actual personality. The spirit must learn to desire, and to progress to higher and better conditions, just as we do on earth.

Do You Mean That We Must Be Re-incarnated Into a New Body?

NO! You can correct the mistakes of earth life, while in the Spirit world, without living on the material plane of life again.

Are Not Your Teachings Allied to Theosophy, Hinduism, Etc.?

Not at all. Such teachings undoubtedly contain some elemental truths, as do all religions, but their application of them differs from ours.

Then You Do Not Believe in "Magic?"

Decidedly not! "Magic" implies something supernatural; we teach that nothing ever happens except by action of natural law.

Then What of Biblical Miracles?

"Miracle" means something done in defiance of Natural

Law, therefore there are no Miracles. The demonstrations you speak of can be manifested today by our Mediums by the application of perfectly natural forces, when the necessary conditions of such manifestations are provided.

Cannot Ill-Disposed Spirits Harm Us?

Only in the same way that unfitting companions can harm you. Your associates have a direct influence on you for good or evil, whether they are in this life or the next. If your own desires are good, nothing but good will come to you.

Can We Choose What Spirits Shall Approach Us?

Certainly. Like attracts like. If you are striving to live a pure, progressive life, you will attract personalities who have like ideals.

Can These Spirits Influence Us Consciously?

Yes, if you desire it. No person, spirit or mortal, can influence by telepathy either for good or ill, anyone who does not in some way invite or permit such influence. You can receive great help from your spirit friends if you ask for it and open your mind to receive it.

In What Form Do Such Influences Come?

In the form of impressions, transferred directly to your soul consciousness. You may not receive them without some training; yet, on the other hand, many people get them continually, but fail to credit them to the true source.

Do These Spirits Come from a Heaven, a Purgatory or a Hell?

We do not believe in such places. Communicating spirits have merely graduated from this form of life into another. That life can be heaven or hell-like, just as each spirit chooses to make it; the same applies to our life here on earth.

Have They Any Special Place of Abode?

They are subject to certain natural laws which regulate the life of each; as the spirit advances in purity and knowledge, its sphere of action widens. The World of Spirit permeates the entire universe—as real and tangible to those who have passed into it as this life and world are to us.

If There Is No Hell How Are the Evil Punished?

Remember, evil comes from ignorance. Hence we do not believe in punishment, but we know that all actions have direct result. Thus acts which injure others react on the doer; sometimes physically, but always spiritually, placing him yet lower in the scale of spiritual development, and retarding his progress and development in Spirit Life. Injurious acts must then be offset by generous, helpful and self-sacrificing deeds and thoughts, which, in turn, exert an uplifting and beneficial effect on the spiritual status and condition of the individual.

Then Even Criminals Can Progress?

Yes. Even the most degraded personality can in time attain to the greatest heights. It is easier, however, to begin progression in earth life.

Then You Do Not Believe in "Vicarious Atonement"?

NO. Each must work out his own salvation; each has an equal opportunity to do this when he shall have atoned for the wrongs and overcome the temptations and allurements to the sense gratifications of earth life.

Will Not Such Teachings Encourage Selfishness and Crime?

Exactly the opposite. When you know, beyond possible doubt, that you cannot escape by "death" from the consequences of your acts, but must surely face them in a short time, you will feel much more disposed to avoid deeds that will injure yourself as well as others.

Judging by This, Spiritualists Must Be Very Moral People.

You will find no more moral or upright people than those who are true believers in spiritualist teachings.

Will Your Teachings Affect Our Political and Social Life?

They will inevitably revolutionize it and purify it for the reasons just given in the several preceding paragraphs. But we aim to build up—not to tear down. Under our philosophy, by the sure, mental, and spiritual growth, development out of improper political and social conditions will be gradually righted requiring no campaign of destruction first.

Selected Poetry

SHE IS NOT DEAD

You call her dead:
You cannot see her in her glad surprise,
Kissing the tear-drops from your weeping eyes;
Moving about you through the ambient air,
Smoothing the whitening ripples of your hair.

You call her dead:
You cannot see the flowers she daily twines
In garlands for you, from immortal vines;
The danger she averts, you never know;
For her sweet care you only tears bestow.

You call her dead:
Vainly you'll wait until the last trump sounds,
Vainly your love entombed beneath the ground!
Vainly in kirk-yard raise your mourning wail!
Your loved is living in some sunnier vale.

You call her dead:
You think her gone to her eternal rest,
Like some strange bird forever left her nest!
Her sweet voice hush'd within the silent grave
While o'er her dust the weeping willows wave.

You call her dead:
And yet she lives and loves! Oh wondrous truth.
In golden skies she breathes immortal youth!
Look upward! where the roseate sunset beams,
Her airy form amid the brightness gleams!

You call her dead:
Oh, speak not thus! Her tender heart you grieve,
And 'twixt her love and yours a barrier weave!
Call her by sweetest name, your voice she'll hear,
And through the darkness like a star appear.

You call her dead:
Lift up your eyes! She is no longer dead!
In your lone path the unseen angels tread!
And when your weary night of earth shall close,
She'll lead you where eternal summer blows.

Elizabeth Barrett Browning,
(*Through a Medium.*)

MY PRAYER

If there be some weaker one,
Give me strength to help him on:
If a blinder soul there be,
Let me guide him nearer thee.
Make my mortal dreams come true,
With the work I fain would do;
Clothed with life, the weak intent
Let me be the thing I meant;
Let me find in thy employ
Peace that dearer is than joy;
Out of self to love be led,
And to heaven acclimated,
Until all things sweet and good
Seem my nature's habitude.

John G. Whittier.

THE HIGHER DUTY

Not for the profit you alone may gain,
  Nor for the peace that hopefulness insures;
Nor for the freedom from the useless pain
  That he who nurses spitefulness endures.

Not merely for the sake of being free
  From profitless regret and needless care;
Not merely for the joy that there may be
  In spurning sorrows that you need not bear.

But for the sake of those who come and go
  Day after day within your little sphere
Forget the fancied ill, the needless woe,
  And speak the helpful, hearty word of cheer.
S. E. Kiser.

ON THE TWENTY-THIRD PSALM

In "pastures green"? Not always; sometimes He
Who knoweth best, in kindness leadeth me
In weary ways, where heavy shadows be.

And by "still waters"? No, not always so;
Oft-times the heavy tempests round me blow.
And o'er my soul the waves and billows go.

But when the storms beat loudest, and I cry
Aloud for help, the Master standeth by,
And whispers to my soul, "Lo, it is I!"

So, where He leads me, I can safely go,
And in the blest hereafter I shall know
Why, in His wisdom, He hath led me so.

MY CREED

I count myself a faithful friend
  Of every child on earth;
I dare not say of one who lives,
  "His was ignoble birth."

For on the brow of every one,
  Though dark that brow may be,
I trace the light of life divine,
  In high or low degree.

Christ said, "Abide ye all in love,"
  Which mandate I revere,
And trust that it may be my guide
  Through all my wanderings here.

All lovely things of good report
  I seek, as flowers the sun;
But more I love the peace of mind
  That comes with duty done.

And, when earth's children seek my aid,
  I hear Love's high command,
And, if within my power to bless,
  I dare not stay my hand.

But, oh! I judge not men by rank—
  I see the balance scale
Of justice in the hand of God,
  And know truth will prevail.

And looking back o'er eons past,
  As through a long, dark night,
I read that what was once called wrong
  Stands now revealed as right.
Belle Bush.

THE SONG OF THE MYSTIC

I walk down the valley of Silence,
  Down the dim, voiceless valley alone.
And I hear not the fall of footstep
  Around me—save God's and my own!
And the hush of my heart is as holy
  As hovers where angels have flown.

Long ago was I weary of voices
  Whose music my heart could not win;
Long ago was I weary of noises
  That fretted my soul with their din;
Long ago was I weary of places
  Where I met only human and sin.

I walked in the world with the worldly;
  And I craved what the world never gave;
And I said: "In the world, each Ideal
  That shines like a star on life's wave,
Is wrecked on the shores of the real,
  And sleeps, like a dream, in a grave."

And still did I pine for the Perfect,
  And still found the False with the true;
I sought 'mid the Human for Heaven,
  But caught a mere glimpse of the Blue;
And I wept when the clouds of the Mortal
  Veiled even that glimpse from my view.

And I toiled on, heart-tired of the Human,
  I moaned 'mid the mazes of men,
Till I knelt, long ago, at an altar,
  And I heard a Voice call me;—since then
I walked down the Valley of Silence,
  That lies far beyond mortal ken.

Do you ask what I found in the Valley?
  'Tis my trysting place with the Divine,
And I fell at the feet of the Holy,
  And about me a Voice said, "Be mine";
And then rose from the depths of my spirit
  An echo, "My heart shall be thine."

Do you ask how I live in the Valley?
  I weep, and I dream, and I pray;
But my tears are as sweet as the dewdrops.
  That fall on the roses in May;
And my prayers, like a perfume from censers,
  Ascendeth to God night and day.

In the hush of the Valley of Silence
  I dream all the songs that I sing,
And the music floats down the dim Valley,
  Till each finds a word for a wing;
That to men, like the dove of the deluge,
  The message of peace they may bring.

But far on the deep there are billows
  That never shall break on the beach,
And I have heard songs in the Silence
  That never shall float into speech,
And I have had dreams in the Valley
  Too lofty for language to reach.

I have seen thoughts in the Valley,
  Ah, me! how my spirit was stirred,
And they wear holy veils on their faces,
  Their footsteps can scarcely be heard;
They pass through the Valley like virgins,
  Too pure for the touch of a word.

Do you ask me the place of the Valley,
  Ye hearts that are furrowed with care?
It lieth afar between mountains,
  And God and His angels are there;
And one is the dark Mount of Sorrow,
  And one the bright mountain of Prayer.
Rev. Abram J. Ryan.

THE VOYAGEUR

There is a plan far greater than the plan you know,
  There is a landscape broader than the one you see,
There is a haven where storm tossed souls may go,
  You call it death—we immortality.
You call it death—this seeming endless sleep,
  We call it birth—the soul at last is free.
'Tis hampered not by time or space—you weep,
  Why weep at death—'Tis immortality.
Farewell, dear Voyageur—'twill not be long,
  Your work is done—now may peace rest with thee.
Your kindly thoughts and deeds—they will live on,
  This is not death—'tis immortality.
Farewell, dear Voyageur—the river winds and turns,
  The cadence of your song wafts near to me.
And now you know the thing that all men learn:
  There is no death: there's immortality.

IMMORTALITY

When coldness wraps this suffering clay,
  Ah, whither strays the immortal mind?
It cannot die, it cannot stay,
  But leaves its darken'd dust behind.
Then, unembodied, doth it trace
  By steps each planet's heavenly way?
Or fill at once the realms of space,
  A thing of eyes, that all survey?

Eternal, boundless, undecay'd,
  A thought unseen, but seeing all,
All, all in earth, or skies display'd,
  Shall it survey, shall it recall;
Each fainter trace that memory holds
  So darkly of departed years,
In one broad glance the soul beholds,
  And all, that was, at once appears.

Before Creation peopled earth,
  Its eyes shall roll through chaos back;
And where the furthest heaven had birth,
  The spirit trace its rising track,
And where the future mars or makes,
  Its glance dilate o'er all to be,
While sun is quench'd or system breaks
  Fix'd in its own eternity.

Above all Hate, or Hope, or Fear,
  It lives all passionless and pure;
An age shall fleet like earthly year;
  Its years as moments shall endure.
Away, away, without a wing,
  O'er all, through all, its thought shall fly;
A nameless and eternal thing,
  Forgetting what it was to die.

Lord Byron.

'I CAN, BECAUSE I OUGHT, AND BY GOD'S HELP I WILL'

When skies hang low, and faith and hope are dim,
And even God's great Love seems far away
A man is tempted very hard to say:
'How can I take life's burden up day after day?'
So these brave words were writ to comfort him,
And heart and mind with noble purpose fill:
'I can, because I ought, and by God's help I will.'

A. P. W.

BLINDNESS

A lark sang his song in the morning light,
Winging his way in happy flight;
"They tell me," he cried, "that the infinite blue
Is filled with new life the whole day through.
And yet, as I soar in the sun's bright glare,
I search in vain to find the air."

Far down in the ocean's briny deep
A fish arose from his lazy sleep;
He wiggled his way from the ooze and the mire
Swimming faster and faster as he rose higher.

"I have heard of the beautiful, crystal sea.
Is there none to tell me where it can be?"

A traveler, bearing a heavy load,
Stopped to rest by the side of the road,
His brow was fanned by the breezes cool,
He drank his fill from a fountain pool.
Then, making his couch on the earth's green sod,
Turned to the sky and cried—
"Where is God?"

E. O. M.

THE OLD CLAY HOUSE

When I am through with this old clay house of mine,
When no more guide-lights through the windows shine,
Just box is up and lay it away
With the other clay houses of yesterday;
And with it, my friends, do try, if you can
To bury the wrongs since first I began
To live in this house; bury deep and forget;
I want to be square and out of your debt.
When I meet the Grand Architect Supreme
Face to face, I want to be clean.
Of course I know it's too late to mend
A bad builded house when we come to the end;
But to you who are building, just look over mine
And make your alterations while yet there is time;
Just study this house, no tears should be shed,
It's like any clay house when the tenant has fled.

I have lived in this house many
    days all alone,
Just waiting, and oh, how I long to
    go home!
Don't misunderstand me, this old
    world divine,
With love, birds and flowers, and
    glorious sunshine,
Is a wonderful place and a wonder-
    ful plan,
And a wonderful, wonderful gift to
    man.
Yet, somehow we feel, when the cy-
    cle's complete
There are dear ones across we are
    anxious to meet;
So we open the books and check up
    the past,
And no more forced balances—this
    is the last.
Each item is checked, each page
    must be clean,
It's the passport we carry our
    Builder Supreme.
So when I am through with this
    old house of clay
Just box it up tight and lay it
    away;
For the Builder has promised when
    this house is spent,
To have one all finished with tim-
    ber I sent
While I lived here in this one. Of
    course it will be
Exactly as I have builded, you see
It's the kind of material we each
    send across,
And if we build poorly of course
    it's our loss.
You ask what material is best to
    select?
'Twas told you long ago since by
    the Great Architect,
"A new commandment I give unto
    you,
That you love one another as I have
    loved you."
So the finest material to send up
    above
Is clear straight-grained timber of
    brotherly love.

        John S. Monck.

BEYOND

It seemeth such a little way to me
    Across to that strange country—
        the Beyond;
And yet, not strange, for it has
    grown to be
    The home of those of whom I am
        so fond,
They make it seem familiar and
    most dear,
As journeying friends bring distant
    regions near.
So close it lies, that when my sight
    is clear
    I think I almost see the gleaming
        strand.
I know I feel those who have gone
    from here
Come near enough sometimes, to
    touch my hand.
I often think, but for our veiled
    eyes,
We should find Heaven right a-
    round about us lies.
I never stand above a bier and see
    The seal of death set on some
        well-loved face
But that I think, "One more to wel-
    come me,
    When I shall cross the interven-
        ing space,
Between this land and that one
    'over there';
One more to make the strange Be-
    yond seem fair."
And so for me there is no sting to
    death,
    And so the grave has lost its
        victory.
It is but crossing—with a bated
    breath,
    And white, set face—a little strip
        of sea,
To find the loved ones waiting on
    the shore,
More beautiful, more precious than
    before.

        Ella Wheeler Wilcox.

THE TIMES

The times are not degenerate.
Man's faith mounts higher than of old.
No crumbling creed can take from the immortal soul the need
Of that supreme creator, GOD.
The wraith of dead beliefs we cherished in our youth
Fades, but to let us welcome newborn truth.

Man may not worship at the ancient shrine,
  Prone on his face, in self-accusing scorn
  That night is past. He hails a fairer morn.
And knows himself a something all divine.
Not humble worm, whose heritage is sin,
But, born of God, he feels the Christ within.

Not loud his prayers as in the olden time,
  But deep his reverence for that mighty force
  That occult working of the great All-Source
Which makes the present era so sublime
Religion now means something high and broad,
And man stood never half to near to God.

      Ella Wheeler Wilcox,
      In Gems from Wilcox.

THE CHEMISTRY OF CHARACTER

John, and Peter, and Robert, and Paul,
God in his wisdom created them all.
John was a statesman, and Peter a slave,
Robert a preacher, and Paul—was a knave.
Evil or good as the case might be,
White, or colored, or bond, or free—
John, and Peter, and Robert, and Paul
God in his wisdom created them all.

Out of earth's elements, mingled with flame,
Out of life's compounds of glory and shame,
Fashioned and shaped by no will of their own
And helplessly into life's history thrown;
Born by the law that compels men to be,
Born to conditions they could not foresee,
John, and Peter, and Robert, and Paul
God in his wisdom created them all.

John was the head and the heart of his state
He was trusted and honored, was noble and great.
Peter was made 'neath life's burdens to groan.
And never once dreamed that his soul was his own.
Robert great glory and honor received,
For zealously preaching what no one believed;
While Paul, of the pleasures of sin took his fill
And gave up his life to the service of ill.

It chanced that these men, in their passing away
From earth and its conflicts; all died the same day—
John was mourned through the length and breadth of the land,

Peter fell neath the lash in a merciless hand—
Robert died with the praise of the Lord on his tongue
While Paul was convicted of murder, and hung.
John, and Peter, and Robert and Paul
The purpose of life was fulfilled in them all.

Men said of the statesman—"How noble and brave!"
But of Peter, alas!—"He was only a slave."
Of Robert—"'Tis well with his soul—it is well";
While Paul they consigned to the torments of hell.
Born by one law through all nature the same,
What made them differ?—and *who* was to blame?
John, and Peter, and Robert, and Paul,
God is his wisdom created them all.

Out in that region of infinite light
Where the soul of the black man is as pure as the white—
Out where the flesh can no longer control
The freedom and faith of the God-given soul—
Who shall determine what change may befall
John, and Peter, and Robert, and Paul.

John may in wisdom and goodness increase.
Peter rejoice in an infinite peace,
Robert may learn that the truths of the Lord
Are more in the Spirit, and less in the word—
And Paul may be blest with a holier birth
Than the passions of man had allowed him on earth.

John, and Peter, and Robert, and Paul
God in his wisdom created them all.
Miss Lizzie Doten.

SUDDENLY REVEALED

A breath of the glory of summer
  Sweeps over my soul today,
Though the winds are searching and tireless
  And the winter skies are gray.
But beyond all the gloom and the shadows
  The fragance and beauty arise,
And I tread—by some magic and music,
  In the pathways of Paradise.
Lilian Whiting.

LEARN TO FORGET

Forget each kindness that you do
  As soon as you have done it;
Forget the praise that falls to you
  The moment you have won it;
Forget the slander that you hear
  Before you can repeat it;
Forget each slight, each spite, each sneer,
  Whenever you may meet it.

Remember every kindness done
  To you, whate'er its measure;
Remember praise by others won
  And pass it on with pleasure;
Remember every promise made
  And keep it to the letter;
Remember those who lend you aid
  And be a grateful debtor.

Remember all the happiness
  That comes your way in living;
Forget each worry and distress;
  Be hopeful and forgiving;
Remember good, remember truth,
Remember heaven's above you,
And you will find through age and youth,
  True joys and hearts to love you.

IF WE KNEW EACH OTHER

"If I knew you and you knew me—
If both of us could clearly see,
And with an inner sight divine
The meaning of your heart and mine—
I'm sure that we would differ less,
And clasp our hands in friendliness;
Our thoughts would pleasantly agree,
If I knew you and you knew me."

THE JOURNEY

I think of death as some delightful journey
That I shall take when all my tasks are done;
Though life has given me a heaping measure
Of all best gifts, and many a cup of pleasure,
Still better things await me further on.

This little earth is such a merry planet,
The distance beyond it so supreme,
I have no doubt that all the mighty spaces
Between us and the stars are filled with faces
More beautiful than any artist's dream.

I like to think that I shall yet behold them,
When from this waiting room my soul has soared.
Earth is a wayside station, where we wander,
Until from out the silent darkness yonder
Death swings his lantern, and cries, "All aboard!"

I think death's train sweeps through the solar system
And passes suns and moons that dwarf our own,
And close beside us we shall find our dearest,
The spirit friends on earth we held the nearest,
And in the shining distance, zone upon zone.

Whatever disappointment may befall me
In plans or pleasures in this world of doubt,
I know that life at worst can but delay me.
But no malicious fate has power to stay me
From that Grand Journey on the Great Death Route.

GOOD DEEDS CAN NEVER, NEVER DIE

Oh, toilers in life's harvest field
Who sow the seeds of truth—yet sigh
That soil is hard, and scant the yield,
Faint not! Good deeds can never die!

What tho' no harvest greets thine eye,
What if thy hands pluck not the fruit,
Tho' strangers share it by and by,
And in thy praises all are mute?

Still true it is, as God is true,
If thy reward be far or nigh,
Do what thy hands may find to do
And lo! Thy deeds shall never die!

Each germ of Truth, each act of Love
Inherent holds a life divine;
And on them ever from above
The dews of heav'n shall fall and shine.

Tho' riches flee, tho' friends depart,
And broken hopes around thee lie,
Still let this message cheer thy heart;
Good deeds shall never, never die!

B. F. Austin.

IMMORTAL LIFE

Immortal Life is something to be earned
By slow self-conquest, comradeship with pain,
And patient seeking after higher truths.
We cannot follow our own wayward wills,
And feed our baser appetites, and give
Loose rein to foolish tempers, year on year,
And then cry, "Lord, forgive me; I believe!"
And straightway bathe in glory. Men must learn
God's system is too grand a thing for that.
The spark divine dwells in our souls, and we
Can fan it to a steady flame of light
Whose lustre gilds the pathway to the tomb
And shines on through eternity; or else
Neglect it till it glimmers down to death,
And leaves us but the darkness of the grave.
Each conquered passion feeds the living flame;
Each well-borne sorrow is a step towards God.
Faith cannot rescue, and no blood redeem
The soul that will not reason and resolve,
Lean on thyself, yet prop thyself with prayer;
(All hope is prayer. Who call it hope no more
Sends prayer footsore forth o'er weary wastes;
While he who calls it hope gives wing to prayer.)
And there are spirits, messengers of love,
Who come at call to fortify our strength;
Make friends with them, and with thine inner self;
Cast out all envy, bitterness and hate,
And keep the mind's fair tabernacle pure,
Shake hands with grief, give greeting unto pain—
Those angels in disguise; and thy glad soul
From height to height, from star to shining star,
Shall climb and claim blest immortality.

Ella Wheeler Wilcox.

GOD GIVE US MEN

God give us men. The time demands
  Strong minds, great hearts, true faith and willing hands;
  Men whom the lust of office does not kill;
  Men whom the spoils of office can not buy;
  Men who possess opinions and a will;
  Men who have honor; men who will not lie;
  Men who can stand before a demagogue
And dam his treacherous flatteries without winking;
  Tall men; sun-crowned, who live above the fog
In public duty and private thinking!
For while the rabble with their thumb-worn creeds,
  Their large professions and their little deeds,
  Mingle in selfish strife; lo! Freedom weeps!
Wrong rules the land, and waiting justice sleeps!

John G. Holland.

FAITH

Just over the river I can see
Loved ones waiting for you and me.
Beautiful, loving, beckoning hand,
Pointing the way to a better land.

Longing to clasp in a loving embrace,
Longing to see us face to face,
Longing to smooth out the lines of care
And tell us the glory awaiting there.

Upward and onward, like the eagle bold,
Soaring away, new lands to behold;
Melodious music now borne to our ears
Tells us we're nearing the heavenly spheres.

No night there and nothing to fear,
The way seems brighter as we draw near.
The portals passed, what shall we see?
What awaits us, you and me?

Rivers like crystal and streets of gold,
Scenes of beauty we shall behold.
Away! Away! from toil and care!
Joy and peace awaits us there.

Visions of grandeur I can see
There, awaiting you and me.
How will they greet us? How shall we know
Those we have loved in the long ago?

Oh, faith divine, all shall be known,
Those we called lost in beauty grown;
We shall see and know them, as of yore,
For love is the same forever more.

Susan I. Boardman.

ON TO THE HEIGHTS

Oh, you who tread the ways of earth,
You are immaculate by birth.

From height to depth, from star to sod,
There is no separate thing from God.

You are in Him, and He in you,
Learn that old platitude anew.

Bask in splendor of the fact,
And live to it in thought and act.

Bask in the knowledge and be free,
All things are yours, for you are He.

He does but manifest through man
The scope and purpose of His plan.

He is the All, and All is One;
We are the beams, and He the sun.

Shine then in glory—light the earth,
You are immaculate by birth.

Discard old creeds of fear and sin,
Live to the God who dwells within.

Absorb the grandeur of the Thought,
For thus may miracles be wrought.

Truth is the lock, and Love the key;
All things are yours to do and be.

Go claim the vast stupendous whole—
On to the heights, Immortal Soul!

Ella Wheeler Wilcox.

THEY WATCH OUR ACTIONS

I do believe the spirits of the dead
  Watch all our actions in this mortal life,
The devious ways by which our feet are led,
  From haunts of peace unto the haunts of strife.

This feeling of communion with departed friends
  Kindles a sense of fellowship divine;
A mutual faith whose quick'ning power tends
  To strengthen hope and harsher thoughts refine.

Memories of loving hearts now stilled forever
  Act as an inspiration unto nobler deeds.
Since we, alas! our earthly ties must sever
  And take the path where the eternal leads.

It may be that the shadows when they darken,
  Are but the prelude to what charms the sight,
And that the deepest silence if we hearken,
  Can soothe us with unspeakable delight.

We are but gropers in Life's fullest meaning,
  And know not where nor whence each footstep leads;
Existence at its best is but a leaning
  On fervent faith—the bulwark of our needs.

Hence the sublimity of ever seeming
  To see the forms we loved and now away;
To think their sight all glorified and beaming
  Still marks our actions thro each mortal day.

For precious as may be living with the living,
  Sharing their aspirations and their sighs,
We are unconscious of the joy in living
  In other realms now veiled from human eyes.

            B. F. D. Dunn.

THE LAW

I ask no good where e'er I go
That I have not by service won;
Nor ask that any joy shall flow
Into my life—if it be none
Have given joy. I cannot draw
From empty store. It is the Law.

I hold this true—it is my creed—
Within me lies my heaven or hell;
It is by my own thought or deed
I build the home where I must dwell.
A marble mansion—tent of straw
I am the builder. It is the Law.

My harvest is the yet to be—
Is that which here and now I sow;
I am uplifted and made free
By that of wrong which I outgrow.
If life lines I distorted draw
I must erase them. It is the Law.

I wear the garments I must wear,
If beggar's rags—or robe of king.
'Tis I the warp and woof prepare,
'Tis I alone the shuttle fling.
No one for me can thread withdraw.
Myself alone. It is the Law.

My Savior is the good I've done
For this alone my heaven is grown.
My crown, the Love that I have won
And deep within is God enthroned.

I to myself will surely draw
That which is mine. It is the Law.

None questions, but the voice within
And my accuse is the soul;
My judge is that stern discipline
That ever seeks to make me whole.
I cannot from this court withdraw.
I must bear witness. It is the Law.

Mary March Baker.

A BUILDER

He was not stylish or rich or great—
Owned neither a mine nor real estate;
But he simply toiled from day to day,
Faithful and honest and brave alway,
Never too tired or poor to give
His best that some other man might live.

His earth-work finished, an angel came,
And softly whispered the old man's name,
And led him to mansions of beauty rare,
Upbuilt by his love and faith and prayer,
And each good deed that in earth-life shone
Was marked above by a shining stone.

Callie Bonney Marble.

PEAKS OF THE IDEAL

High to our lifted eyes the tall peaks seem;
But when by rugged pains with toil extreme
And one sharp struggle we have reached the crest,
Another rises higher far whose breast,
The while we struggle up the first ascent,
Lay all unseen with clouds and shadow blent
Then fiercely set, we ceaseless strive and climb,
But ever, ever higher far, Sublime
Ideal, do thy tow'ring ramparts rise,
And as we climb, still lift to higher skies.

Joseph I. C. Clarke.

THE CREED

Whoever was begotten by pure love,
And came desired and welcomed into life.
Is of Immaculate Conception. He
Whose heart is full of tenderness and truth,
Who loves mankind more than he loves himself,
And cannot find room in his heart for hate,
May be another Christ. We all may be
The Saviours of the world, if we believe
In the Divinity which dwells in us
And worship it, and nail our grosser selves,
Our tempers, greeds, and our unworthy aims upon the cross.
Who giveth love to all,
Pays kindness for unkindness, smiles for frowns,
And lends new courage to each fainting heart,
And strengthens hope and scatters joy abroad,
He, too, is a Redeemer, Son of God.

Ella Wheeler Wilcox,
In Gems from Wilcox.

LIFE

"To be, or not to be," is not "the
 question."
There is no chance of Life. Ay,
 mark it well!—
For Death is but another name for
 change.
The weary shuffle off their mortal
 coil,
And think to slumber in eternal
 night;
But, lo the man, though dead, is
 living still;
Unclothed, is clothed upon, and his
 Mortality
Is swallowed up in Life.

THE OTHER WORLD

It lies around us like a cloud—
 A world we do not see,
But the sweet closing of an eye
 May bring us there to thee.

Its gentle breezes fan our cheeks
 Amid our worldly cares;
Its gentle voices whisper love
 And mingle with our prayers.

Sweet hearts around us throb and
 beat,
 Sweet helping hands are stirred,
And palpitates the veil between
 With breathing almost heard.

The silence—awful, sweet, and
 calm—
 They have no power to break;
For mortal words are not for them
 To utter or partake.

And in the hush of rest they bring,
 'Tis easy now to see,
How lovely, and how sweet a pass,
 The hour of death may be.

To close the eye, to close the ear,
 Wrapt in a trance of bliss,
And gently dream in loving arms,
 To swoon to that—from this.

Scarce knowing if we wake or
 sleep,
 Scarce asking where we are,
To feel all evil sink away,
 All sorrow and all care.

Sweet souls around us! Watch us
 still,
 Press nearer to our side,
Into our thoughts, into our prayers,
 With gentle helpings glide.

Let death between us be as naught,
 A dried and vanished stream,
Your joy be the reality,
 Our suffering like the dream.

H. B. Stowe.

WAITING

Serene I fold my hands and wait,
 Nor care for wind, or tide, nor
 sea;
I rave no more 'gainst Time or
 Fate,
 For lo! my own shall come to me.

I stay my haste, I make delays,
 For what avails this eager pace?
I stand amid the eternal ways,
 And what is mine shall know my
 face.

Asleep, awake, by night or day,
 The friends I seek are seeking
 me;
No wind can drive my bark astray,
 Nor change the tide of destiny.

What matter if I stand alone?
 I wait with joy the coming years;
My heart shall reap where it hath
 sown,
 And garner up its fruit of tears.

The waters know their own and
 draw
 The book that springs in yonder
 height.
So flows the good with equal law
 Unto the Soul of pure delight.

The stars come nightly to the sky;
  The tidal wave comes to the sea;
Nor time, nor space, nor deep, nor high,
  Can keep my own away from me.

Serene, I fold my hands and wait,
  Whate'er the storms of life may be,
Faith guides me up to heaven's gate,
  And love will bring my own to me.
          John Burroughs.

SOME TIME

Some time, when all life's lessons have been learned,
  And sun and stars forevermore have set,
The things which our weak judgment here has spurned—
  The things o'er which we grieved with lashes wet—
Will flash before us out of life's dark night,
  As stars shine most in deeper tints of blue;
And we shall see how all God's plans were right,
  And how what seemed reproof was love most true.

And we shall see that while we frown and sigh,
  God's plans go on as best for you and me;
How, when we called, He heeded not our cry,
  Because His wisdom to the end could see;
And, e'en as prudent parents disallow
  Too much of sweet to craving babyhood,
So God, perhaps, is keeping from us now
  Life's sweetest things, because it seemeth good.

And if some time, commingled with life's wine,
  We find the wormwood, and rebel and shrink,
Be sure a wiser hand than yours or mine
  Pours out this potion for our lips to drink;
And if some friend we love is lying low,
  Where human kisses cannot reach his face,
Oh! do not blame the loving Father so,
  But bear your sorrow with obedient grace.

And you shall shortly know that lengthened breath.
  Is not the sweetest gift God sends His friend,
And that sometimes the sable pall of death
  Conceals the fairest boon His love can send;
If we could push ajar the gates of life,
  And stand within, and all God's working see,
We could interpret all this doubt and strife,
  And for each mystery could find a key.

But not today. Then be content, poor heart;
  God's plans, like lilies pure and white, unfold;
We must not tear the close-shut leaves apart;
  Time will reveal the calyxes of gold.
And if through patient toil we reach the land
  Where tired feet, with sandals loose may rest,
When we shall clearly know and understand,
  I think that we shall say that "God knew best."

THE WELL-SPENT DAY

"If we sit down at set of sun
And count the acts that we have done,
  And, counting find
One self-denying act, one word
That eased the heart of him who heard,
  One glance most kind,
That fell like sunshine where it went,
Then we may count that day well-spent."

A PRAYER

Teach me, Father, how to go
Softly as the grasses grow;
Hush my soul to meet the shock
Of the wild world as a rock;
But my spirit, propt with power,
Make as simple as a flower;
Let the dry heart fill its cup,
Like a poppy looking up;
Let Life lightly wear her crown,
Like the poppy looking down,
When its heart is filled with dew,
And its life begins anew
Teach me, Father, how to be
Kind and patient as a tree;
Joyfully the crickets croon
Under shady oak at noon;
Beetle, on his mission bent,
Tarries in that cooling tent;
Let me, also, cheer a spot,
Hidden field or garden grot—
Place where passing souls can rest
On the way and be their best.
        Edwin Markham.

"IN MEMORIAM"

How pure at heart and sound in head,
  With what divine affections bold
  Should be the man whose thought would hold
An hour's communion with the dead.

In vain shalt thou, or any, call
  The spirits from their golden day,
  Except, like them, thou, too, canst say,
My spirit is at peace with all.

They haunt the silence of the breast,
  Imagination calm and fair;
  The memory like a cloudless air,
The conscience as a sea at rest.

But when the heart is full of din,
  And doubt beside the portal waits,
  They can but listen at the gates,
And hear the household jar within.
        Alfred Tennyson.

EMANCIPATION

Why be afraid of death, as though your life were breath?
Death but anoints your eyes with clay. Oh, glad surprise!
Why should you be forlorn? Death only husks the corn.
Why should you fear to meet the thresher of the wheat?
Is sleep a thing of dread? Yet sleeping you are dead
Till you awake and rise, here or beyond the skies.
Why should it be a wrench to leave your wooden bench?
Why not with happy shout run home when school is out?
The dear ones left behind! O, foolish one and blind,
A day and you will meet—a night and you will greet.
This is the death of death, to breathe away a breath,
And know the end of strife, and taste the deathless life,
And joy without a fear, and smile without a tear
And work, not care to rest, and find the last the best.
        Maltbie D. Babcock.

GLAD TIDINGS

From hill and valley ringing,
  From prairie-land and street,
Rich melody is bringing
  Glad tidings fair and sweet;
Friends join from realms immortal,
  And signal from Love's day—
"Rejoice, beyond Deaths portal,
  The mists have cleared away."

We turn from old time errors,
  To sing with friends above:
"Death is not King of Terrors,
  But Lord of Life and Love;
No cypress wreath is twining
  O'er forms of earth-worn clay,
For spirit faces shining,
  Have cleared the mists away."

Of old they told the story
  Of resurrection dawn:
We feel its daily glory,
  And watch the coming morn.
Hail! Souls from isles supernal,
  Who still in spirit say:
"Life wears Love's crown eternal,
  The mists have cleared away."

          C. Fannie Allyn.

WE THANK THEE

We thank Thee for the beauty which the morning shows,
We thank Thee for the sweetness of the night's repose.

We thank Thee for the glory of the rising sun,
We thank Thee for the twilight when the day is done.

We thank Thee for the noon-day and the clearer view,
We thank Thee for the darkness— then the stars shine through.

We thank Thee for the fragrance of the flow'ry spring.
We thank Thee for the bounty which the summers bring.

We thank Thee for the splendor of the autumn's glow,
We thank Thee for the sparkle of the winter snow.

We thank Thee that each season of the day and year
Makes thy graceful tenderness faithfully appear.

          Napoleon S. Hoagland.

THE SPIRIT'S FAREWELL

Rest, tired clay; I've done with thee.
How long I've worn thee as the captive
Wears the dragging chain, that fetters
Him to earth. What pains and weakness
Have we known together, what strife,
What weariness, what sad impotency.
Yet thou hast served me well—hast
Been a willing slave to task-master stern.
Who no pity showed to thee, for oft, when
E'en existence was a battle, did this
Same eager, tireless spirit gird thee on
To yet greater effort and endeavor.
Handful of dust, once vitalized,
Thou oft hast longed for the embrace
Of the bridegroom, Death; hast thought
It would be sweet to lie down in
His restful arms; thou feelest them now,
Rest in thy bridal bed, from whence
No morrow makes to toil, no restless
Spirit goads thee to action, evermore.
O friends, dear friends, all and each,

Why look ye on this wornout frame
That can not give the love ye
    crave?
Its passing set me free, rejoice in
    this,
Its poor mortal eyes and ears no
    longer
Veil from me sweet sights and
    sounds.
I see you all—I sense your Love—
    I know.
O Father—Now I know and thank
    Thee
For Thy greatest gift—blest im-
    mortality.
                  S. C. Clark.

HAUNTED HOUSES

All houses wherein men have lived
    and died
    Are haunted houses. Through
        the open door
The harmless phantoms on their
    errands glide,
    With feet that make no sound
        upon the floor.

There are more guests at table than
    the host
    Invited; illuminated hall
Is thronged with quiet, inoffensive
    ghosts
    As silent as the picture on the
        wall.
      *   *   *   *   *
The spirit-world around this world
    of sense
    Floats like an atmosphere, and
        everywhere
Wafts thro' these mists and vapors
    dense
    A vital breath of more ethereal
        air.
        Henry W. Longfellow.

ANGELS' TWILIGHT BELL

There has come to my mind a
    legend, a thing I half forgot,
And whether I read it or dreamed
    it; ah, well, it matters not.
It's said that in heaven at Twilight
    a great bell softly swings,
And man may listen and harken to
    the wonderful music that
    rings,
If he puts from his heart's inner
    chamber all the passion, pain
    and strife,
Heartaches and weary longing, that
    throb in the pulses of life;
If he thrusts from his soul all
    hatred, all thoughts of wicked
    things,
He can hear in the holy twilight
    how the bell of the angel
    rings.
And I think there is in this legend,
    if we open our eyes to see,
Somewhat of an inner meaning, my
    friend, to you and to me;
Let's look in our hearts and ques-
    tion, "Can pure thoughts en-
    ter in
To a soul if it be already the
    dwelling of thoughts of sin?"
So, then, let us ponder a little; let
    us look in our hearts and see,
If the twilight bell of the angels
    could ring—for you and me.

AWAY

I cannot say, and I will not say
That he is dead. He is just away!
With a cheery smile and wave of
    the hand,
He has wandered into an unknown
    land.
And left us dreaming how very fair
It needs must be, since he lingers
    there.
And you—O you, who the wildest
    yearn
For the old-time steps and the
    glad return—
Think of him faring on, as dear
In the love of There as the love of
    Here.
Think of him still as the same, I
    say,
He is not dead—he is just away.
        James Whitcomb Riley.

THE INEVITABLE

I like the man who faces what he must
  With step triumphant and a heart of cheer;
Who fights the daily battle without fear,
Sees his hopes fail, yet keeps unfaltering trust
That God is God; that somehow, true and just
  His plans work out for mortals; not a tear
  Is shed when fortune, which the world holds dear,
Falls from his grasp; better, with love, a crust
Than living in dishonor; envies not,
  Nor loses faith in man; but does his best
Nor ever mourns over his humbler lot,
  But with a smile and words of hope, gives zest
To every toiler; he alone is great,
Who by a life heroic conquers fate.
              Sarah K. Bolton.

FOOTSTEPS OF ANGELS

When the hours of day are numbered,
  And the voices of the night
Wake the better soul that slumbered,
  To a holy, calm delight;

Ere the evening lamps are lighted,
  And, like phantoms grim and tall,
Shadows from the fitful firelight
  Dance upon the parlor wall;

Then the forms of the departed
  Enter at the open door;
The beloved, the true hearted,
  Come to visit me once more;

With a slow and noiseless footstep
  Comes that messenger divine,
Takes the vacant chair beside me,
  Lays her gentle hand in mine.

And she sits and gazes at me.
  With those deep and tender eyes,
Like the stars, so still and saint-like
  Looking downward from the skies.

Uttered not, yet comprehended,
  Is the spirit's voiceless prayer,
Soft rebukes, in blessing ended,
  Breathing from her lips of air.

O, though oft depressed and lonely,
  All my fears are laid aside,
If I but remember only,
  Such as these have lived and died!
              H. W. Longfellow.

Published by permission of Houghton, Mifflin and Company

THE BUILDERS

All are architects of Fate,
  Working in these walls of Time;
Some with massive deeds and great,
  Some with ornaments of rhyme.

Nothing useless is, or low;
  Each thing in its place is best;
And what seems but idle show
  Strengthens and supports the rest.

For the structure that we raise,
  Time is with materials filled;
Our todays and yesterdays
  Are the blocks with which we build.

Build today, then strong and sure,
  With a firm and ample base;
And ascending and secure
  Shall tomorrow find its place.

Thus alone can we attain
  To those turrets, where the eye
Sees the world as one vast plane
  And one boundless reach of sky.
              H. W. Longfellow.

Published by permission of Houghton, Mifflin & Company.

KNOWLEDGE

I tell you the shadows are growing thinner
Between this world and the world of the dead;
And only the fool cries "FOOL" or "SINNER"
To one who looks into the life ahead,
I tell you the curtain is being lifted—
The silence broken, the darkness rifted—
And Knowledge is taking the place of Faith
On the vast subject DEATH.

Yes:—Now in the place of Faith comes Knowledge
For the Soul of the Race is awake to Truth,
And it rests no longer on school or college
Or the crude concepts of the world's first youth.
From a larger fountain our minds are drinking—
The deep, high Source of divinely thinking—
And searching for GOD in the heart of MAN
It is so we are learning the plan.

Yes:—Searching for GOD in the heart of a Brother
And not on a far-away throne above,
Is a surer method than any other
Of finding the Center of Truth and Love.
And out of that Center a voice is crying
That our Dead are not, in their low graves, lying
But are living and loving us, close and near
So long as we hold them dear.

Yes:—Living and Loving and trying to guide us—
Invisible helpers, by GOD'S sweet will
Who ofttimes move through the day beside us,
But aiding us most when our minds are still.
I tell you the curtain is being lifted,
The silence broken, the darkness rifted—
And KNOWLEDGE is taking the place of FAITH
On that vast subject, DEATH.
Ella Wheeler Wilcox.

THE ADVENTURE BEAUTIFUL

Today the journey is ended;
  I have worked out the mandates of fate;
Naked, Alone, Undefended,
  I knock at the uttermost gate.

Lo! The gate swings wide at my knocking;
  Across endless reaches I see
Lost friends, with laughter come flocking
  To give a glad welcome to me.

Farewell! The maze has been threaded;
  This is the ending of strife;
Say not that death should be dreaded,
  'Tis but the beginning of life.
Selected.

ONLY

Only a touch, a whisper,
I said would banish unrest;
Only a glance from the eyes I love
Will make my life so blest.
And I heeded not there that the sun shone fair
And the wind came out of the west.

Only the old-time music
Of the songs that my spirit caught
Only a vanished presence,
Only a loving thought,
And I failed to hear the music near,
With which the air was fraught.
Lilian Whiting

THERE IS NO DEATH

There is no death! The soul lives on for aye,
  'Tis but a changing to another sphere,
E'en though the body passes back to earth
  The soul lives on, in spirit life, as here;
It will expand, and thrive, and ever grow,
  And still retain its influences o'er
Those left on earth, until they, too, shall go
  To join those who have merely gone before.
There is no death! 'Tis but a higher growth,
  The soul continues to another scene
Devoid of all encumbrances of earth,—
  Shorn of all pain and suffering so keen;
And while we'll miss its daily presence here,
  And from its sweet companionship are torn,
We will be blessed, inspired and comforted
  By its o'er shadowing love, in heaven born.
There is no death! 'Tis but a change of form,
  Enabling the soul to reach its own,
And there expanding with each cycle made
  As it ascends near to the heavenly throne;
Our life on earth is but a transient stay,
  As onward to a future life we tread,
And, having gained experience of earth,
  We then pass on with those the world calls dead.
There is no death! For life can never die,
  Life is as potent as the truth itself,
It lives forever, through eternity;
And when, in turn, the summons comes to us
  To pass unto the land that lies beyond,
We should not sorrow, but should e'en rejoice
  That we've gained our freedom from earth's bond.

I. C. I. Evans.

THE SPIRIT OF NATURE

I have come from the heart of all natural things,
  Whose life is from the Soul of the Beautiful springs;
You shall hear the sweet waving of corn in my voice,
  And the musical whisper of leaves that rejoice,
For my lips have been touched by the spirit of prayer,
  Which lingers unseen in the soft summer air;
And the smile of the sunshine that brightens the skies,
  Hath left a glad ray of its light in my eyes.

There is something in Nature beyond our control,
  That is tenderly winning the love of each soul;
We shall linger no longer in darkness and doubt,
  When the Beauty within meets Beauty without.
Sweet Spirit of Nature! wherever thou art,
  O, fold us like children, close, close to thy heart;
Till we learn that thy bosom is Truth's hallowed shrine,
  And the Soul of the Beautiful is —the Divine.

Lizzie Doten

THE RAINBOW BRIDGE

'Twas a faith that was held by the
    Northmen bold
In the ages long, long, ago
That the river of death, so dark
    and cold
Was spanned by a radiant bow;
A rainbow bridge to the blest abode
Of the strong gods—free from ill
Where the beautiful Urda fountain
    flowed
Near the ash tree Igdra sill.

And they held that when, in life's
    weary march
They should come to the river
    wide,
They would set their feet on the
    shining arch
And would pass to the other side.
And they said that the gods and the
    heroes crossed
That bridge from the world of
    light,
To strengthen the soul when its
    hope seemed lost
In the conflict for the right.

Oh beautiful faith of the grand old
    past!
So simple, yet so sublime;
A light from that rainbow bridge is
    cast
Far down o'er the tide of Time.
We raise our eyes, and we see
    above,
The souls in their homeward
    march;
They wave their hands and they
    smile in love,
From the height of that rainbow
    arch.

We know they will drink from the
    fountain pure
That springs by the Tree of Life;
We know that their spirits will rest
    secure
From the tempests of human strife;
So we fold our hands, and we close
    our eyes
And we strive to forget our pain
Lest the weak and the selfish wish
    should arise
To ask for them back again.

The swelling tide of our grief we
    stay,
While our warm hearts fondly
    yearn,
And we ask if over that shining
    way
They shall nevermore return.
Oh we oft forget that our lonely
    hours
Are known to the souls we love,
And they strew the path of our life
    with flowers
From that rainbow arch above.

We hear them call, and their voices
    sweet
Float down from the bridge of
    light,
Where the gold and crimson and
    azure meet
And mingle their glories bright.
We hear them call, and the soul
    replies
From the depths of the life below,
And we strive on the wings of faith
    to rise
To the height of that radiant bow.

Like the crystal ladder that Jacob
    saw
Is that beautiful vision given,
The weary pilgrims of earth to
    draw
To the life of their native heaven.
For it's better that souls should
    upward tend
And strive for the victors crown,
Than to ask the angels their help to
    lend,
And come to man's weakness down.

That rainbow bridge in the crystal
    dome
O'er a swiftly flowing tide,

Is the shining way to the spirit home
That lies on the other side.
To man is the tempest cloud below
And the storm wind's fatal breath,
But for those that cross over that shining bow
There is no more pain nor death.

Oh, fair and bright does the archway stand,
Through the silent lapse of years,
Fashioned and reared by no human hand
From the sunshine of love and tears.
Sweet spirits, our footsteps are nearing fast
The light of the shining shore;
We shall cross that rainbow bridge at last
And greet you in joy once more.

Lizzie Doten.

AFTER THE STORMY WEATHER
A Poem for Decoration Day

It's after the stormy weather—camp's still and the fighting done;
And we're closer, thank God, together in the joy o' that battle, won
Under the flag united—friendly as friends may be,
The man who marched with Sherman and the man who followed Lee.

It's after the stormy weather. See now where the skies blend blue,
And light the stars of the flag that waves so splendidly over you!
The battle thunders have died away—the folds of the flag float free,
And fainter now are the echoes of the guns from over the sea.

After the stormy weather! Peace on the plains and hills;
No crimson drops on the daisies, no red on the rippled rills.
Only one thought for the country: "Waves the flag from shore to shore;
Wrongs righted, and love-united, we are brothers forevermore!"

One thought! Let the rivers sing it where the dreaming valleys sleep!
One thought! Let the winds proclaim it far up on the wooded steep!
Thrilled to the stars in music; after the rough ways trod,
We are all at home in the country under the smile of God!

Frank L. Stanton.

SWEET REST AT LAST

Sweet rest at last!
  At last the hands are folded
    Upon a pulseless breast,
And a soul tired, of earth's great burden weary,
    Hath found sweet rest.

Sweet rest at last!
A long and faithful worker
    On life's broad beaten road,
Reaching the confines of a life immortal,
    Lays down his load.

Sweet rest at last!
No longer thorns are pressing
    Upon a careworn brow,
But from the heavens a fadeless crown of blessing
    Rests on it now.

Sweet rest at last!
No more earth's fretting discord
    Disturbs the holy calm.
But angel choirs chant to the
    list'ning spirit
    Their peaceful psalm.

    Sweet rest at last!
We clasp our hand in silence,
    And only hope to be
Some time with those who enter at
    the portal,
    And heaven to see.

    Sweet rest at last!
Some time, amid the realms of fade-
    less beauty

Earth's toils and sorrows past,
Find, with the dear ones who have
    gone before us,
    Sweet rest at last.

INDEX

A

	Page
Admission to Fellowship Service	90
American Flag, The	87
American Flag, Pledge to	87
Flag, Salute to the	87
Anniversary Service	78

B

Barrett, Harrison D.	10
Bible References and Spirit Manifestations	163
Burial Service (for General Purposes)	106
Burial Service for Child	110
By-Laws on "Gratitude Day"	83

C

Clairvoyance, Definitions of	114
Constitutional Convention	15
Conventions of N. S. A.	16-19

D

Declaration of Principles	34
Definitions Adopted by N. S. A. C.	34-37
Definitions of Clairvoyance	114
Definitions of Prophecy	154
Definitions of Religion	113
Definitions of Spiritual Healing	116

F

Fellowship Service	90
Foretelling, Definition of	154
Foreword	13
Founders Day Service	96

G

	Page
"Gratitude Day" Service	83

H

Healing (Bible References)	162
Healing, Definitions of	116
Healing, Suggestions as Aid to	117
Hiding Man's Divinity	45-73
Hydesville Cottage, Picture of	75-76
Hymns—	
America	89
Star Spangled Banner	87
America, the Beautiful	88

I

Interpretation of Principles	35-36
Inspirational Speaking	154
Invocations and Readings	46-73

L

Liberty and the Law	170
Lyceum Burial Service	110
Lyceum, Spiritualist Progressive	172
Lying Spirits (Bible Reference)	162

M

Man—Limitless	146
Marriage Service No. 1	100
Marriage Service No. 2	103
Ministry of Angels (Bible Reference)	163
Modern Spiritualism	74

N

Naming Service for Children	92-95
Naturalness of Mediumship	40

O

	Page
Objects of Spiritualism	39
Officers and Trustees, N. S. A. C.	20-33

P

Patriotic Service	86
Philosophy of Spiritualism	41-44
Brotherhood of Man	41
Children Grow in Spirit World	44
Earthly Deeds Affect Spirit	43
Evolution of Man	41
Happiness Attainable by All	44
Infinite Intelligence	41
Inspiration Perpetual	44
Man's Duty on Earth	41
Man's Individuality	42
Man's Moral Status After Death	43
Matter and Spirit Co-related	42
Mediumship	44
Music and Harmony	42
Objects of Spiritualism	39
Purpose of Spirit Life	44
Spirit Communications	43
Spirit Manifestation	43
Universe, Origin of, etc.	41
What Spiritualism Is and Does	
Poetry Selected	190
A Builder	202
Actions, They Watch Our	
Adventure Beautiful, The	209
After the Stormy Weather	212
Angels' Twilight Bell	207
A Prayer	205
Away	207
Beyond	195
Blindness	194
Builders, The	208
Emancipation	205
Faith	200
Footsteps of Angels	208
Glad Tidings	206
God Give Us Men	199
Good Deeds Can Never Die	198
Haunted Houses	207
I Can, Because I Ought, And By God's Help I Will	194
If We Knew Each Other	198
Immortality	193
Immortal Life	199
In Memoriam	205
Knowledge	209
Learn to Forget	197
Life	203
My Creed	191
My Prayer	190
On the Twenty-Third Psalm	191
On to the Heights	200
Only	209
Peaks of the Ideal	202
She Is Not Dead	190
Some Time	204
Suddenly Revealed	197
Sweet Rest at Last	212
The Chemistry of Character	196
The Creed	202
The Higher Duty	191
The Inevitable	208
The Journey	198
The Law	201
The Old Clay House	194
The Other World	203
The Rainbow Bridge	211
The Song of the Mystic	192
The Spirit's Farewell	206
The Spirit of Nature	210

	Page
The Times	196
The Voyageur	193
The Well-Spent Day	205
There Is No Death	210
They Watch Our Actions	201
Waiting	203
We Thank Thee	206
Prophecy	156

Q

	Page
Questions and Answers About Spiritualism	178
Quotations—Selected Prose	119-145
Abbott, James	144
Anthony, Saint	128
Austin, Dr. B. F.	129 and 143
Barrett, Harrison D.	134
Barwise, Hon. Mark A.	139
Beecher, Henry Ward	123
Boscowan, Prof.	119
Buddhist Scriptures	120
Cato	120
Cicero	122
Chambers, Dr. Robert	129
Clark, Dr. Adam	128
Clark, Susie C.	141
Colville, W. J.	136
Davis, Andrew Jackson	123
Dickens, Charles	129
Doten, Lizzie	125
Doyle, Arthur Conan	144
Ecclesiastes	122
Edmunds, J. W.	123
Erwood, Will J.	125 and 140
Favre, M. Leon	126
Flammarion, Camille	136
Francis, John R.	137
Fuller, Dr. Geo. A.	141
Garrison, William Lloyd	128

	Page
Goetz, Elizabeth Harlow	141
Grimshaw, Thomas	139
Hardinge, Emma (now Britten)	125
Haweis, Rev. H. R.	130
Hawthorne, Nathaniel	125
Holmes, Oliver Wendell	132
Hawthorne, Nathaniel	125
Homer	119
Hugo, Victor	127
Hull, Moses	126
Ignatius	128
Irving, Washington	131
Jesus	122
Kant	132
Kates, George W.	140
Kiddle, Prof. Henry	132
Quotations—Selected Prose, Continued	
King, Starr	124
Lacordaire, Father	132
Lillie, Mrs. R. S.	133
Lockwood, Prof. W. M.	142
Lodge, Sir Oliver	143
Longley, Mary T.	140
Loveland, Prof. J. S.	135
Mahomet	124
Massey, Gerald	129
Maynard, Nettie Colburn	123
Milton	122
Murray, Rev. W. H.	130
Newton, J. F.	45
Ocharowicz	131
Paine, Thomas	124
Parker, Theodore	127
Peck, Prof. W. F.	135
Peebles, Dr. J. M.	132
Plato	121
Plutarch	122
Pythagoras	120

Richmond, Coral L. V. 135
Russegue, Helen L. P. 133
Sardou, Victorien 130
Sargent, Epes 131
Savage, Minot J............. 125
Schlesinger, Julia (now Garison) 134
Seneca 120
Smith, Charles R............ 11
Socrates 120
Sprague, E. W...... 136 and 145
Stowe, Harriet Beecher..... 131
Tertullian 128
Tuttle, Hudson 124
Twing, Carrie E. S.......... 137
Vanderbilt, Mary S......... 142
Varley, C. F................ 126
Wallace, Alfred Russell..... 126
Warne, Dr. George B.. 10 and 137
Whitwell, Joseph P......... 11
Wiggin, Fred A............. 142
Wood, Henry 143-144
Zend-Avesta 119

R

Readings 46-73
  Death, The Gateway to Life 54
  Divinity of Nature.......... 58
  Inspiration 64
  Into the Silence............ 62
  Life's Anchor 50
  Power of Spirits............ 48
  Road to Happiness.......... 60
  Self-Reliance 52
  True Religion 56
  What Is Spiritualism?...... 38
  Wisdom and Love.......... 66
  Easter 68
  Thanksgiving 70

Christmas 72
Religion, Definitions of........ 113
Religious Liberty 170

S

Self Culture, Suggestions for.. 147
Selected Poetry 190
Services, Anniversary 74
  " Burial for General Purposes 106
  " Burial for Children.. 110
  " Fellowship 90
  " "Gratitude Day" 83
  " Invocations and Readings 46-73
  " Naming of Children. 92-95
  " Marriage No. 1...... 100
  " Marriage No. 2...... 103
  " Patriotic 85
Spirit Manifestations of the Bible 158
  Clairaudience 161
  Clairvoyance 161
  Dreams 162
  Healing 162
  Independent Voices 162
  Inspiration 159
  Levitation 161
  Lying Spirits 162
  Magnetized Articles, Healing by 162
  Materialization 159
  Mediumship 159
  Ministry of Angels.......... 160
  Physical Manifestations 158
  Speaking in Unknown Tongues 159

	Page		Page
Speaking Through Trumpets	162	Trance Mediumship	153
Spiritual Body	158	Trance Mediumship Not Hurtful	153
Trance	151	Trance Speaking	151
Visions	162		
Voices, Independent Spirit	162		
Writing, Direct Spirit	160		
Spiritual Healing	162		
Suggestions as Healing Agency	117		
Suggestions for Self Culture	147		

T

Things to Cultivate and Things to Avoid 148

V

Visions (Bible References) 163
Voices, Independent Spirit (Bible References) 163

W

Warne, Dr. Geo. B........... 10
What Spiritualism Is and Does 38